ARCHIE JACKSON
THE KEATS OF CRICKET

ARCHIE JACKSON

THE KEATS OF CRICKET

David Frith

with a Foreword by
Harold Larwood

PAVILION
MICHAEL JOSEPH

To the memory of my mother

Published in Great Britain in 1987 by
Pavilion Books Limited
196 Shaftesbury Avenue, London WC2H 8JL
in association with Michael Joseph Limited
27 Wrights Lane, Kensington, London W8 5TZ

First published in a limited edition in 1974

© David Frith 1974

Revised edition © David Frith 1987

British Library Cataloguing in Publication Data

Frith, David, *1937–*
Archie Jackson: the Keats of Cricket.
1. Jackson, Archie
I. Title
796.35′8′0924   GV915.J/

ISBN 1–85145–119–6

Printed and bound in Great Britain by Anchor Brendon

CONTENTS

ILLUSTRATIONS

Sweating it out at The Oval
Jackson about to be caught by Larwood at Headingley
Bradman and Jackson batting at The Oval
Jackson swinging Peebles away
Archie, back in Australia, visiting his mother
Australia v West Indies, Sydney, February 1931
A recuperating Jackson reunited with Bradman and Fingleton
A brave pose at Calvary Hospital, Adelaide, in 1932
Archie and his fiancée Phyllis Thomas
A letter to a friend
The crowd outside the Jackson home before his funeral
Bill Hunt tending his old pal's grave, forty years on

All the photographs, with the exception of that of Jackson batting against Victoria in 1927–28, which was loaned by Michael Down, are from the author's collection.

ACKNOWLEDGEMENTS

A biography is seldom the work of one alone. Archie Jackson's story took shape only after fellow players, friends and relatives had added large measures of personal data to the basic material accessible in books and newspapers.

Bill Hunt's wholehearted assistance is, I think, clearly evident in the narrative. So too is that of Archie Jackson's surviving sisters, Miss Peggie Jackson and Mrs Jean Bruce, and of Mrs Phyllis Kennedy (née Thomas).

Among contemporary players in Sydney, Alan Kippax, whose death was sadly recorded only a few months later, gave generously of his memories and time, as did Bertie Oldfield, Frank Buckle, H. L. Hendry, and Bill O'Reilly.

The vigilance of Pat Mullins, Australia's leading collector of cricket literature, ensured the unearthing of several other useful morsels.

Though Adelaide proved beyond reach, letters to Clarrie Grimmett brought painstaking replies, gratefully received.

Archie Jackson's friend in Hampshire, Harry Mills, provided a most important insight in the correspondence retained over forty years. Harry read this book in type-script, but died suddenly before its publication. He was an especially good man, so like his cricketing friend from Sydney.

Among pre-war England cricketers, R. E. S. Wyatt, Herbert Sutcliffe, Leslie Ames, Ian Peebles, and George Geary spoke glowingly in concord of the young Australian, and I am indebted to all of them for important substantiations.

A good deal of fresh material has been incorporated into this new edition, and Michael Down's loan of the photograph of Archie batting against Victoria at Sydney in 1927–28 is especially appreciated.

But my warmest appreciation goes to Harold Larwood for writing the foreword. As he says, he does not often commit pen to paper, but here was a request he would not refuse. It was the conclusive tribute to the man whose story you are about to read.

Guildford, 1987   DAVID FRITH

In that short life
there was abundant action
and a full measure of joy

A. G. Moyes

FOREWORD
by Harold Larwood
former Notts and England fast bowler

When first approached to write a foreword I politely refused. However, it was explained by this persistent fellow that he had spent considerable time researching on a cricketer he believed I must have admired. I asked who this could be? His reply left me humbled, for it was none other than Archie Jackson.

It hit me just about as hard as Archie did that day at Adelaide in 1929 when, in his first Test innings for Australia, with 97 runs against his name and having had his back to the wall, he cover-drove me to bring up his hundred. That ball was delivered as fast as any I had ever bowled previously.

That glorious stroke has lived in my memory to this day for its ease and perfect timing. I am sure that few among the many thousands present sighted the ball as it raced to the boundary.

I personally had a very great admiration for Archie, and I am sure we 'Poms' counted him as one of us. He never failed to congratulate the bowler or fieldsman whenever he was dismissed by a good ball, and at the same time he would be the first to let you know when he thought you were not bowling so well. He would say: 'You must have had a late one last night, Harold!'

He was always friendly, no matter the tenseness of the

situation – you just had to find a place in your heart for a fellow like him. The respect he showed for others grew on you.

I remember once, in England during the 1930 series, in scoring 73 at The Oval in the fifth Test, he was taking quite a physical beating. As he came down the wicket to level a high spot or two he said: 'Well, Harold, it's only a game, but what a grand one we're having today! I hope you're enjoying our battle as much as those spectators seem to be. You know, you've hit me almost as many times as I've hit you! I wish you'd drop one a little off line occasionally.'

I never knew him to flinch or complain at any time.

No, Archie Jackson, like his hero Victor Trumper, was born to be great, and great he was, for he received the same respect from us 'Poms' as from his own team.

But we had a feeling that something was amiss with this young fellow in 1930. Those of us who were closely associated with him knew that the English climate did not suit him; he was not himself. He still batted with the same charm that only he was capable of, but it was apparent that he was not the same Archie as that of 1928–29.

One of my most cherished possessions to this day is a personal telegram sent to me by Archie while undoubtedly a very sick boy in Brisbane; it congratulated me on my bowling in that controversial Test of 1933. At the time he must have been very close to meeting his Maker, but he was still conscious enough to remember an old friend.

I remember also a number of us Englishmen visiting Archie in the private hospital in Brisbane one afternoon after practice before the fourth Test. It was the last time we were to see him, for during the final stages of that Test match he passed away. We felt the depression that was cast over the ground when early that morning the news came through that Archie was no more.

It was hard to believe. We knew that our loss was Australia's too. Privileged were those who had known him. I for one could never forget Archie Jackson.

HAROLD LARWOOD

CHAPTER ONE

IN THE LINE OF TRUMPER

There is a love – and usually a sadness – at the heart of a cult. Victor Trumper was the first tragic hero of Australian cricket. His failing health robbed him of untold hours in the sun, and though his death in 1915 did not shorten his international career, the loss of his maturity, the years of fullness when a veteran spreads himself in relaxation and reminiscence, was grieved. He was humble and kind; he deserved a long life. All who knew him believed this.

The dreamy Alan Kippax, who mirrored Trumper, had an extensive and loyal following during the 1920s and 1930s, but in an era when his finesse was mistrusted by Test selectors he left his lyrical style in the memory and assumed, in the eyes of the world, a stature undeservedly less than major; the book of figures tells but one side of his story.

At his zenith Kippax welcomed into the ranks of the New South Wales team a slender, athletic lad who, though never having seen Trumper, possessed all the comely movement and keenness of eye of Sydney's God of Cricket. His exceptional talent had proclaimed itself at a precocious age, and cricketers all around him watched expectantly as Archie Jackson's promised gift grew to fulfilment.

This was the beginning of a cult. Men of all ages who saw him never forgot him, and a generation later they still held his banner. All those who had made his acquaintance shared the desire to be regarded as his intimate friends.

Jackson was to bear uncomplainingly an insidious sickness that racked him for years. He disdained treatment, perhaps in disbelief, perhaps in valiant optimism.

When – the last of the line – he died at 23, cricket's transition from an aesthetic exercise to a purely mathematical strategy was under way. His influence was missed very seriously. No spectator could ever have watched him late-cut or advance to the drive without having to stifle the temptation to imitate.

In such premature death there is a danger that the legend becomes gilded; that is not the case here. A wealth of evidence substantiates the expectation and eventual manifestation of Jackson's splendour.

The wider tragedy, apart from the pity that avid England only ever saw a faint shadow of the man, is that during the businesslike 1930s there was no Archie Jackson to provide a model and an inspiration to youthful cricketers in both countries. Kippax played halfway through the decade and made many graceful hundreds, but his peak had been around 1926, when 21 of his 22 Australian caps were still to come. Two savage blows to the head had also upset him irretrievably.

The decade – for Australia – was dominated by Bradman, Ponsford, Woodfull, and McCabe, all except the last having a predictable near-infallibility. Jackson might have continued to add a touch of Dresden.

Or he might have tightened up as the seasons passed, unable, even by repeating his follies, to recapture his artistic youth. But I doubt it.

A telephone call got things under way: 'Bill Hunt, the cricketer?'

'That is so.'

I introduced myself. 'I understand from Alan Kippax that you were a close friend of Archie Jackson's?'

'May I say that no-one knew him better.'

So began the reconstruction of a career. I pored over Bill's scrapbooks and filled notebooks as reminiscence played itself out. He introduced me to Jackson's two sisters and they in turn referred me to his former fiancée. I began to see the subject from other angles.

Walking the streets of Balmain, standing outside his childhood home, talking with elder sister Peggie in the house in Drummoyne to which the family later graduated, finding his grave at the Field of Mars Cemetery, seeking out old team-mates and adversaries – I found that the young man's spirit lived still.

Unexpectedly, I obtained access to a number of Jackson's letters, most of them full of hope and rationalisation, written with candour to some of his friends during the last five years of his life.

Then, finally, Bill arranged to show a brief cine-film of Archie Jackson playing his range of strokes on the No. 2 Ground at Sydney over forty summers before. There he stood, bat held high on the handle, his cap-peak drooping like a guardsman's.

The casual elegance of his leg glances, the whalebone suppleness of his wrists as he steered the ball square and backward, the lightness of footwork, the ballet-like inclination of the body as he cover-drove – the artistry, enhanced by a beguiling self-consciousness, burned an impression on my mind.

The demonstration had been more than adequate. The only surviving film of Trumper is an abrupt and cruel misrepresentation of his magical technique, but for five enchanted minutes I had had the great good fortune to see a faithful image of his spiritual descendant.

I found myself aligned with all those thousands who, having seen Jackson batting, sighed for more when he was dismissed.

CHAPTER TWO

EMIGRANT BOY

Archie Jackson, like Adam Lindsay Gordon, Billy Hughes ('the Little Digger'), Russell Drysdale, Frank Ifield, Patrick White, Charlie Bannerman and a number of other famous Australians, was born on the opposite side of the world. The Jackson family lived at 1 Anderson Place, Rutherglen, south of Glasgow, when Archibald arrived on September 5, 1909. Margaret and Alexander already had two daughters: Lil, aged five, and Peggie, three.

'Sandy' (father Alex) was manager of a brickworks at Belvedere. He had been taken to Australia in a sailing ship with his parents when he was twelve, but returned to Scotland five or six years later. Now, as a 41-year-old working man with responsibilities, he eyed NSW thoughtfully once more. Times were tough in Glasgow.

Thus Sandy struck out again for Australia and paved the way for Mrs Jackson and the children to follow eighteen months later. *Themistocles,* soon to be sunk in the First World War, landed them safely in Sydney on August 1, 1913.

The family set up house in the tilting, rambling old waterside suburb of Balmain: at 14 Ferdinand Street, a small, cosy, iron-roofed, terraced house, built in two storeys of brick, with a laced-iron balcony. It still stands.

After the War the family was completed by the birth of

Jeanie, a precious sister for the other girls, and for Archie, whose early disapproval at not getting a baby brother soon evaporated.

'Don't leave her outside in the pram,' he often pleaded. 'Someone'll take her away!'

He spoilt Jeanie more with each passing year.

There was never much money about, and Archie had to make do with one pair of pants for the greater part of his boyhood, the sole advantage being that his mother could withhold them whenever he was forbidden from going out.

But the home felt secure and was happy. Sandy worked at Cockatoo Dockyard and gave the rest of his time to his family. He put rubber bars on Archie's worn shoes and they served as soccer boots; he made a bat for him to use in the street games, both by day and under the illumination of the gas lamps – not merely a carved plank, but a realistically-shaped implement with a *cane handle*. He earned in return a tender adulation.

'Isn't that your boy, Sandy?' said a workmate one afternoon as a rowing boat floated past the Dock with a small figure lying face-down to avoid recognition. The lad explained that evening that he had only wanted to see his Dad at work. The punishment for truancy was not severe.

The parents were usually good-humoured, too, when he returned with a sackful of apples filched from the orchard up at Mars Field. Other times he amused himself by riding the laundry cart through the narrow Balmain streets.

A well-remembered crisis was when he fought with school-mate Tommy Thompson through four consecutive afternoons before sister Lil felt bound to tell Mum, who went straight down to Birchgrove Park to break it up.

He was no angel. But he was loving, and he was greatly loved.

When Archie's school, Birchgrove, played cricket against Smith Street, he met Bill Hunt and began a lifelong friendship. They became pals during the 1920–21 season, when J. W. H. T. Douglas's MCC team were moving round Australia from one defeat to the next at the mighty hands of Warwick Armstrong, Jack Gregory, Ted McDonald, Charlie Macartney, Herbie Collins, Charlie Kelleway, 'Nip' Pellew, Arthur Mailey – a formidable assembly of skills.

Archie idolised certain cricketers from each side, and he and Bill – when they were not satisfied to play 'numbers cricket' out of the hymn-book in Bible class – had a resourceful manoeuvre for getting to the Sydney Cricket Ground. They 'wagged' school at lunchtime, hopped on to a Wood Coffill hearse on its way back to the city, and used their threepence lunch money to get into the ground, where they quenched their thirsts at the bubbler at the base of the Hill, watched the international stars at play – wishing they could be out there too – and went hungry.

After play they usually hitched a ride on the meat wagon back to Balmain, where the mothers strove to fill their bellies.

'They talk about pollution in the 1970s!' said Bill Hunt fifty years later. 'In those days the people of Balmain used to spread coal dust on their bread!'

Archie's special capabilities in the field of sport soon became obvious. He was selected for NSW Schoolboys at both soccer and cricket, travelling to Melbourne under Wendell Bill's captaincy for the summer game and impressing the cricket fraternity there, and distinguishing himself in the inter-state soccer carnival as a slight but highly-skilled centre-forward adept at flicking the ball over the head of a charging opponent and running round him.

He played against South Australia twice, Victoria, and Queensland, scoring thirteen goals.

The Jackson home was hardly a hundred yards from Birchgrove Park, where Balmain District Cricket Club played each Saturday. The captain was whimsical Arthur Mailey, plumber, cartoonist, writer, indefatigable and extravagant spinner of the ball for NSW and Australia.

Soon after little Archie entered the lower grades, playing in short trousers and appearing too fragile for exposure to adult fast bowling, Mailey wrote prophetically of him in the local paper:

Balmain has developed a young batsman who may take a big part in Australian cricket. The club officials must be congratulated upon their success. May other clubs have the same good fortune. It is not often that we see a fifteen-year-old batsman – for he was fifteen two weeks ago – with such a splendid variety of strokes as A. Jackson, the boy cricketer, who scored 71 for Balmain against the juniors last Saturday.

As a rule, in a boy so young, there is that apparent anxiety that affects his cricket, and periods of cramped play occasionally are seen. But Jackson just moves along, flicking this ball past point or through the covers, and turning the next sweetly to leg with the grace of a master. As a second line of defence, his legs are always in a handy position, but it is refreshing to know that he intends to use his bat whenever possible.

I am not going to compare him with the glorious Victor Trumper at this stage, but if a wealth of common sense and ability is an asset, then this boy's future is assured. He played with the Balmain 2nds last season, and should find a place in the first team this year.

8

As a second string in his bow he has the moral support of twelve juvenile barrackers, whose loyalty and devotion are remarkable. And who would not give something to listen in at some ice cream shop in Balmain while the hero tells of his wonderful experiences of the day's play against the 'big' bowlers?

Young Jackson is going to wreck the averages of some bowlers. Fortunately, I'm in the same team, so it won't be mine.

The grade captains at Balmain were fighting over him by now, and it was felt by the seniors that the cries of 'Too young!' by the lower grades were nothing more than an attempt to keep the budding genius for themselves. When he was blooded in the first team in 1924–25, a season when Australia was in the fervid grip of another MCC tour, Archie, at fifteen years and one month, was thought to be the youngest debutant ever in first-grade cricket.

He had been batting with such style and ease in fourth, third, and second grades that crowds were drawing away from the senior matches to see him – a tiny performer whose pads flapped halfway up his thighs and whose flagging strength as the innings wore on found compensation in pliant wristwork, dancing feet, and uncanny timing and placement. Spectators at Birchgrove, seeing him strain under the weight of a man's bat, once even clubbed together to buy him a Harrow-sized bat.

He lived for cricket. If the silent films at the local were disappointing he would go home before the end and, standing on the dining-room table, practise his footwork against the sideboard mirror – an old C. B. Fry pastime.

One of his problems was sleepwalking – especially, it was noted, during the cricket season. His father found it advisable to tie up the bedroom door handle to save him

9

from falling over the lace ironwork which encased the balcony.

Earlier, before the risk had been realised, he had actually spent the hotter, steamier nights on that balcony, where a bed could be wedged. His somnambulations often led him down to the kitchen late at night: he would slump into the rocking chair while his mother, who knew perfectly well how to handle him, carried on with her ironing. After a few minutes of unreal conversation she would direct him back to bed, and loud snoring soon came as an assurance that the wanderings were at an end for one more night.

Archie ('The Champ') and Bill ('The Count') enjoyed their schooldays and made the best of them, for they tended to end early in Balmain. Archie, having passed his Qualifying Certificate at fourteen, had gone to Rozelle School; but a year later he was a schoolboy no more. The family needed his financial help, and he was eager to pay his way.

Joining Jackson (no relation) & McDonald, he worked distractedly in the warehouse until cricket got the better of him. As his career developed and his absences became more frequent he was compelled to leave, and soon found himself working for Alan Kippax in his sports shop in Martin Place. The business had got away to a very sound start in 1926 after the Australian selection had surprisingly overlooked Kippax for the tour of England; now, after inviting the boy to call in, he opened a bank account for him and put him to work.

Kippax was to have a profound influence on Jackson as his mentor and captain in NSW matches. He gave him quiet guidance, encouragement, and, as his employer, generous time to practise and to play during the week.

Kippax played for Waverley, Jackson for Balmain, on

the other side of town. But the Fates had brought them together, and Victor Trumper's ghost must have smiled.

Another benefactor had been Herbert Vere Evatt, then a young lawyer living in Balmain, and later to become one of Australia's most distinguished men: Chief Justice of NSW, Leader of the Federal Parliamentary Labor Party, Cabinet Minister, and President of the United Nations Assembly. Dr Evatt and Arthur Mailey saw to it that poverty never prevented a Balmain boy from having cricket equipment and being a paid-up member of the club.

The debt to these men and to sportsmaster John Mitchell was never forgotten by five boys from Rozelle School who all became first-class cricketers: Archie Jackson, Bill Hunt, Syd Hird, Dudley Seddon and Dick Nutt.

In 1923–24 Archie made three centuries for Rozelle, and his average of 69 made no allowance for several retirements. He was also an 'exceedingly fine slip field, and useful change bowler' who claimed on one exhilarating occasion 6 for 1 including a hat-trick.

He and Bill enjoyed their greatest success against Auburn School, whom they dismissed for 7, Jackson 4 for 2, Hunt 6 for 1, with four byes! Syd Hird, who later lived in South Africa, remembered Archie taking 8 for 2: 'yours truly claimed the other two for two runs.' He also recalled a 'tour' up to the Hawkesbury River, when the little Balmain cricketers were greeted almost with disdain. So they batted until almost 500 was on the board, and Archie was one of the centurymakers. They then dismissed the locals for 11 and 13 (or thereabouts).

Every evening the gang played in Birchgrove Park, where a rule had to be introduced to stop Archie batting forever: compulsory retirement at 100. Consequently Archie, upon reaching the nineties, would stonewall. The answer had to be – and was – strategic overthrows to see him to three figures.

At Birchgrove, where Archie had captained the team at the age of twelve, making four centuries and taking 8 for 12 and 7 for 11, another sportsmaster often predicted that he would be playing for Balmain first team at seventeen, NSW at eighteen, and Australia at nineteen. The forecast was bold, yet, as it happened, safe. He was playing for the State at seventeen.

It was the same sportsmaster Byrnes who had felt Archie's absence through illness so severely in a crucial school match that he had authorised the boys to call round and plead with Mrs Jackson to let her son play. He was allowed to bat with a runner, made a few runs, and the Premiership was won.

He could not stay away from the game; his team-mates could never accept his absence with equanimity. This impatience in later years was to hasten his death.

In his first season in Balmain 1sts, following a moderate start and reversion to the 2nds, he was brought up again in an emergency and secured his place for the rest of his years.

He was showing a solid defence and command of every stroke even if he was able to exert precious little physical power. His highest was a fighting 41 not out in two hours, and he finished second in the averages with 30.75. He was now equally at home on turf pitches.

He had batted fearlessly against the fireballs of Jack Gregory and Jack Scott and the briskness of Sam Everett and Charles Kelleway, and the conclusion was inescapable: the 'babe' had an uncanny instinct for batting. His afferent nerve (eye to brain) and efferent nerve (brain to limb) were abnormally sharp, as they are in all top sportsmen.

Nor did he merely allow his skill to evolve only in match play. He practised at Birchgrove Oval from five o'clock till dusk and was back for more in the clear morning air at half-past-seven before setting off to work.

He was a keen reader, not only of Edgar Wallace and travel tales, famous lives and boy's adventure, but of cricket books – particularly those recording the great England v Australia battles.

Most of his dreams must have been of the 'big cricket' which everyone in the district was now predicting for him, though on one sleepwalk he was climbing up to place files on an hallucinatory shelf, thinking himself to be at the warehouse. His father grabbed him as he was about to topple over the balcony. That would have been that.

As the 1925–26 season opened he was just sixteen. At first he struggled, and there were those who began to wonder if the frail prodigy had been but a momentary deception of Nature. Then the runs came.

Opening against Western Suburbs, he carried his bat doggedly for 58 out of 103 and made 61 in the second innings. His 88 against University was dazzling. And his first century in first-grade cricket was recorded against St George, a club due the following season to enlist a promising colt (D. Bradman) from the country.

After Jackson's beautiful 129 there was a collection among the onlookers for which he shyly expressed his gratitude. There was jubilation in his home town.

At the end of the season he stood impertinently atop the Balmain averages with the considerable aggregate of 670 runs at almost 40. He had taken another step up the ladder in being selected for NSW 2nd XI against Victoria, making a modest 25 and 30 while the senior side in Sydney were piling up 708 (Kippax – overcoming a supposed nervous disposition yet again – making 271 not out).

To top off the summer he escaped the hurly-burly of first-grade cricket at Easter when 20 Balmain players and supporters travelled to Goulburn in *three* cars! Little Jackson extricated himself from the vehicle and made 59 and 74, and stroked 35 against Kenmore.

Home-life continued as full of affection and animation as ever, with the unchangeably Scots parents quietly proud of their budding champion of a son and the sisters contesting his company. Dad, a physical-fitness crank who had an incurable weakness for impromptu chin-ups in the kitchen, was incapable of noisy pride, yet no father was ever more gratified at a son's progress. This was the boy who, at the age of two and a half, had attracted a crowd at a Scottish holiday resort when giving a display of his virtuosity with a football.

'I don't want your money!' the infant had bawled indignantly when his audience showed its appreciation.

The family never ceased using certain peculiarly Scottish expressions even after many years of Balmain life, though Archie, as he grew up, spoke with care and ever-improving expression. Remembering him in the age of television, his sisters 'heard' him whenever English actor Roger Moore ('The Saint' and 'James Bond') uttered his lines.

His love of reading matured into an interest in writing, evidenced firstly in his personal letters and later in his newspaper articles. J. C. Davis, Australia's authoritative cricket journalist, felt he could have become a writer of some distinction, and not necessarily only on cricket, when his playing days were past.

Davis had first seen him batting when his fame was nothing more than local. A friend, having watched schoolboy Archie a few days previously, had urged Davis to cast an eye over a 'young Trumper'. They went to Balmain.

'He looks to be Victor reborn,' said the friend.

Davis, mesmerised, was bound to agree.

Yet if Trumper's mantle became an impediment to him, Archie Jackson was never to show it.

CHAPTER THREE
THE BLOODING

England took the Ashes from Australia in 1926. In a famous match at The Oval, where the honours were spread chiefly among the ancient Wilfred Rhodes, the new hope Harold Larwood, and the supreme Hobbs and Sutcliffe, England finally buried Australia's dominance after four post-war series.

If not in mourning, Australia entered a period of anxious contemplation as the household names were lost one by one: Collins turned to full-time bookmaking, Bardsley went into a sort of retirement, Johnny Taylor, troubled by war injuries, concentrated on his dental practice, Arthur Richardson moved to what was then cricket obscurity in Western Australia, and, most regretted, Macartney, 'the Governor-General', retired after one further home season.

With several of the Test tourists delaying their return to Australia for the 1926–27 season, eyes turned to the youngsters, and in the laudable Australian tradition the NSW selectors searched for good cricketers without concerning themselves too much with the degree of dampness behind the prospects' ears.

Archie Jackson, Balmain's pride, grasped his chance with a sensational start to the grade season. His 111 against St George took only two hours. Against Western Suburbs he scored 143, this time his effortless leg-side play catching attention. It was noted that he had gone easy for three innings 'on account of a slight attack of ill-health', but after the triumph against Wests he hit yet another century, 158 in better than even time against Mosman.

There was no surprise when he was in the side selected to play Queensland in Brisbane, a city of destiny for him.

He had had to negotiate the ordeal of a trial match at Sydney under the probing gaze of the past masters. As the aspirants went through their paces there was much shaking of heads: 'then a fresh-faced, almost wisp of a boy, stepped through the gate of a fateful click which is music to the reminiscent champions.'

Two charming cuts that beat deep third man laid an instant stillness over the ground, then there was a chatter and shifting in chairs that betokened recognition of perfect strokeplay. It was 'the advent of a master'.

He went on to 53, retired, and each stroke – the persuasive leaning drive where the ball did its own work, the leg glance, soundless in its delicacy – 'brought the joyous light to sparkle in the eyes of the veterans.'

His debut match in first-class cricket was Queensland's first in Sheffield Shield competition, and, to the relief of many, they performed splendidly, failing by only eight runs to make 400 for victory. The three big men of Queensland cricket all stamped themselves on the match: Leo O'Connor, tragically run out for 196 to end it, Cecil Thompson, 134 in the first innings, and Ron Oxenham, seven wickets.

Jackson, true to a disconcerting habit, failed in NSW's first innings, but compensated with a second effort of 86, run out. His skipper, Kippax, made a century in each innings by way of encouragement.

His one identifiable fault was, and continued to be, an occasional failing outside the off stump. Like Kippax, he was prone to dab late and wilfully at the away-swinger. If it came off, this lazy and now obsolete stroke sent the ball careering past the ankles of helpless slips fielders and into the boundary before third man could do anything about it. If it failed it looked dismal. He often murmured 'Don't cut, Archie' during the early stages of his innings.

But the cries that the youngster should put more 'hammer' into his strokes were in vain. It would have been against Nature; he had a confessed love for applying the greatest velocity to the ball with the minimum of effort.

The selectors, it is said, were certain of his greatness from the start, and he was never really on trial. Quite to the contrary: he was to be permanently in the side, short of a calamity.

In the return match with Queensland, at Sydney, NSW were salvaged in the first innings by a Macartney century, but two hundreds by O'Connor won the match for Queensland, who compiled 577 in their reply. That they were eventually set as many as 300 to win was due to some fine batting in the second innings by Norman Phillips, Alan Kippax (who now had four centuries in five innings), and Jackson, who scored 100 delightful runs.

He added 100 for the fourth wicket with Kippax, and, although the 36-year-old Queensland captain, Leo O'Connor, was carried shoulder-high from the field at the end and joy was boundless in the visitors' dressing-room, there was immense satisfaction around Sydney that 'Second-Innings' Jackson had supplanted speculation with achievement.

The climax of his century was nerve-racking. He was 99 when last man McNamee came in to face the final ball of an over. He survived, and Archie took strike, needing a tremblingly important single. Four times he drove off the meat of the bat – straight to fieldsmen who refused to fumble. Then, as the clock struck noon, he managed to push an off-drive through, and his feet skimmed on down the pitch to the far end as the shrill voice of the crowd rose almost as a national hymn.

He had passed his novitiate.

Just before Christmas he travelled with NSW on the southern tour, which this time produced two matches quite as extraordinary as they were typical of Australian first-class cricket's capacity for the grotesque. At Adelaide, South Australia made 500, to which NSW replied with 341 – Jackson 4. By the time NSW batted again they needed an astronomical 446 to win.

They made them. T. J. E. 'Tosser' Andrews hit 126, Phillips 52, Kippax 42; but the vital contributions came from Morgan (116) and Jackson (56 not out). They added 130 for the sixth wicket, and with twenty-year-old Jim Hogg as his seventh-wicket partner, Jackson tapped Arthur Richardson through mid-on and scampered the winning run.

It had been the most significant two hours he had yet spent at the wicket, and as he waited for his partner to join him and support him through the embarrassment of the return to their jubilant team-mates, he might well have reflected that the victory was all the more praiseworthy for having been achieved against two very fine spinners: A. J. Richardson and C. V. Grimmett, who had secured only a wicket apiece in 64 overs.

The excitement was short-lived. At Melbourne, after being dismissed for 221, they fielded, eagerly and tirelessly, be it stated, for ten and a half hours while Victoria amassed a world record 1107 runs.

Ponsford (352) narrowly missed Clem Hill's record 365 not out, bemoaning his 'bad luck' when he finally played on; an unprecedented 573 runs were hit on the second day; Hendry (100) and Ryder (295) both, according to the former, hitting with gay abandon in the half-hope of being caught, succeeded only in hitting huge fours and sixes; Andy Ratcliffe, undeterred by a couple of costly errors, kept wicket keenly throughout; and Arthur Mailey's characteristic summary became a national joke: 'It was rather a pity Ellis got run out at 1107, because I was just striking a length. Very few chances were given, but I think a chap in a tweed coat dropped Jack Ryder near the shilling stand!'

Mailey took 4 for 362 off 64 overs, all bowled into the wind, though his stoicism and tactical beliefs were seen as misguided by some. If he had bowled *with* the wind, they said, he would have placed the onus on the batsmen hitting against it.

Fifty thousand cheered the thousand up and the passing of the previous world record of 1059 – both events carried by the ebullient Jack Ellis, who bellowed 'Long live Victoria!' as he bolted the vital runs.

Archie Jackson, having made 4 in the first innings and run himself ragged in the field, dredged up the stamina to score an unbeaten 59 as NSW subsided to 230 all out.

'Glad to have seen it all,' was the general summary among spectators, 'but not again. Bad for cricket.'

On New Year's Day Jackson played for E. L. Waddy's team against Northern Tasmania at Launceston. This time it was the turn of the New South Welshmen to make, and not chase, runs. Kippax made 132, Waddy 112, Sullivan 124, and Jackson 160.

An official approached Kippax during the tea interval and asked if he and Jackson, who was still batting with him, might help the scorers to differentiate between them. Could one of the batsmen possibly wear a coloured waist sash?

It would look rather absurd, thought Kippax, but yes, of course, they would co-operate: Archie would wear the sash!

A week later, back on the mainland, Jackson made his first duck in big cricket, caught behind.

South Australia piled on the runs in their second innings, tiny Karl Schneider's 146 remarkably containing only three fours, and NSW found themselves needing 547 for victory. They had made 446 to win the Adelaide match. What was another hundred?

But there was to be no second miracle. 'Perker' Lee's off-breaks accounted for 5 for 36. NSW's 206 owed much to the trusty Kippax, who made 52 ... and his seventeen-year-old protégé, 104 not out.

The score was 37 for 4 when Jackson went in. Tearaway Jack Scott was bowling with rare devil and the wily Grimmett was wheeling away nefariously. In the face of this Jackson stroked 50 in even time. His century partnership with Kippax came in 71 minutes.

The fledgling then hedged, creeping unsteadily to 97 before sliding a beautiful drive through the covers for two. Then there was an overthrow and he had his first century on the Sydney Cricket Ground. Fieldsmen, sharing his thrill, ran to congratulate him.

The journalist A. R. B. Palmer was struck by Archie's classical style during this innings, noting how deceptive was his reach: 'He steps forward to cover-drive – not far enough is one's first impression; he'll lift that ball – but his wrists come into play, and the stroke is perfectly balanced and true ... the bat seems to be a whip in his hands.'

Now he had absolutely no chance of escaping the brand of 'second-innings batsman'. In five matches he had made 17 runs in the first innings and (for twice out) 405 in the second.

It was time for another sensation, and once more Victoria supplied it. Coming to Sydney without Ponsford, Woodfull or Ryder, far from making a thousand runs, they were cast aside by Ray McNamee and Charles Macartney for 35. The pitch was no fun to bat on, even if it had been when NSW started the match: Kippax occupied the crease for less than four hours for 217 runs.

This was Macartney's final Shield match, though a month later he took a more remunerative final bow at Sydney in a benefit match played between the 1926 Australian XI and The Rest. The omitted Kippax made a hundred against the Test team that for personal and obvious reasons gave him intense satisfaction, and in the second innings, on his way to 51, he passed a thousand for the season.

The Australian XI made 533, Woodfull and Andrews getting hundreds and Ponsford registering his sixth in successive matches. But for all the runs, it was universally accepted that Jackson's 32 in the next innings was a prettier effort than any.

He eventually fell to his old tutor and mentor, Arthur Mailey, caught-and-bowled. There was some doubt about the catch, and Mailey frowned tentatively towards the umpire. But when he turned Jackson had gone, satisfied he was out.

In first-class cricket Jackson had made 500 runs at an average of 50, and in spite of having missed several grade matches he finished with 870 runs for Balmain, scoring, in twelve innings, five centuries and a 96 (which included a rare six onto the embankment). This total put him at the top of the Sydney grade aggregates – the first Balmain player to win the honour. His aggregate stood as a club record for 53 years, until Mike Gatting made 878 in 19 innings in the 1979–80 season.

Jackson had been an object of fascination to the great as well as the humble onlookers. Clem Hill was quick to see him as the great discovery, 'the biggest find since Ponsford'. He liked the sparkling footwork, his movement in the field, reminiscent of Johnny Taylor. He had watched him closely enough even to notice that his toes turned in slightly as he walked.

Another of his idiosyncrasies was the wearing of his sleeves almost down to the wrists. What very few knew was that this was not in imitation of Kippax, nor solely to prevent sunburn on his Celtic skin. He was troubled by psoriasis, a skin inflammation of which even now the fundamental cause is unknown. Archie Jackson was perhaps over-conscious of the scaly blemishes on his back and arms. So well did he conceal the problem that the majority of his team-mates were unaware. Frank Buckle, a fine batsman early in the century and later manager of a NSW side that included Archie, recalled how he would shower privately at the end of the day, and often left a wide trail of talcum powder in his wake.

Charles Kelleway, in assessing the exciting new batsman, was guarded – even critical. He disliked the flourish, especially in his back-play, when the bat often came down fractionally late; he wished he would not be so 'cramped with copying other batsmen's styles. These might be above or even below his standard.' The summary came as a relief: 'These flaws are only trifles and, therefore, easily rectified, but need to be pointed out by the right person.'

Alan Kippax, one suspects, was not everywhere considered to be the right person. Yet Jackson, being a child of Nature like Denis Compton a decade later, had to bat in a certain manner and no other.

He had absorbed the advice of many along the line:

George Blakemore at Birchgrove School, Jack Mitchell at Rozelle School, Arthur Mailey, with his insight and good humour, and Jimmy Searle at the SCG nets – Searle, who gave his heart and soul to his 'Colts' after suffering the unenvied and probably unique distinction of having shattered a bone in his leg in colliding with the gutter while fielding at the Sydney ground in 1889.

But of them all it was the example of Alan Kippax, ever near, that had the greatest effect. So uncannily similar were they that A. B. R. Roche, a grazier from Goodooga who befriended Archie and led him into the world of literature, art and the theatre, was moved to write (perhaps to argue the point unto himself) his personal analysis of the two most absorbing batting styles to be seen in Australia between the two wars:

> Alan, after he took block, shuffled forward in front of the wicket a fraction of an inch at a time till the ball was delivered. Archie never moved. Archie in his forward driving strokes used his whole body from toes to head, and he only straightened up after contact. His leg glance and square cut and late cut were altogether his own. Heard Bradman once say 'How do you manage that leg glance?' The answer was: 'I don't know.' All his strokes were natural and *his* only. He never did Kippax's chop. You ask any Queensland cricketer.

CHAPTER FOUR

TO NEW ZEALAND

He was eighteen at the start of the 1927–28 season, and had there been a Test series almost certainly he would have taken part in it. As it was, he had a sniff of international cricket early in the season in the match between NSW and the homecoming New Zealanders, who had just surprised England with their batting strength. That the bowling was unpenetrative was underlined by the State side as it accumulated 571. Jack Gregory smashed a century before lunch and added 262 with Andrews in two dazzling hours. Later Kippax and Jackson raised a century stand in the astonishing time of 36 minutes, and were not separated until they had put together 176. Each made a century (Archie's coming in 71 minutes) and NSW won by ten wickets.

Jackson was quickly into his stride. This hundred followed an innings of 108 against Wauchope during a country tour with Kippax's side, and he also hit a two-hour century off North Sydney, for whom Bill O'Reilly had just come up from the country to enlist. It was one of the uncommon occasions when 'Tiger' failed to take a wicket.

In November Jackson accompanied the NSW team to Brisbane and was among the early calamities as his side lost 4 for 17. There was no play on the second and third days, and though the visitors had to follow on, there was no time for Queensland to force outright victory.

A fortnight later he was again eased out of the picture, firstly by a boil on the knee, then by two early dismissals against Victoria. The knee became troublesome during the journey across the continent, and his withdrawal from the South Australia match allowed young Don Bradman to be included for the first time. He scored 118.

In Melbourne the stumbling block was the ubiquitous Ponsford who, having started the season with 133 and a world record 437, now made 202 (and was to follow it with 336 in the next match), thus having broken the heart of every Sheffield Shield bowler in the land.

The aged Ironmonger and Blackie (both 45) finished the job when NSW batted, though McNamee had covered himself in glory for the vanquished by taking 7 for 77. The match was further notable for Woodfull (with his own score 191) making the first second-innings declaration in the history of the competition.

Home in Sydney, Jackson remained in the doldrums during the New Year match with Queensland. It was a remarkable contest, Kippax scoring 315 not out and later enforcing the follow-on. So well did Queensland bat this time that when NSW tried for the 227 for victory they were hard put to stave off defeat: Otto Nothling used a rain-damaged pitch to advantage and had 5 for 39 when time ran out.

Next day NSW went straight into the return with South Australia, and if Archie Jackson was anxious and impatient for a return to form, he kept it to himself. Bill Hunt recalled how, on the infrequent occasions when Archie lifted a ball, it seemed to go to hand; but he was never one for making excuses.

'What did that one do, Archie?' invariably brought a stock reply: 'Got a good'un!'

Any good'uns he received in this SA match he dealt with ably enough – in both innings. Kippax decided he should open, rather than sit watching his fellows make runs, himself dying a thousand deaths. He made 131 and 122, and returned to the headlines with a smiling vengeance.

The first innings took four hours, the second an hour less; and once more the Sydney crowd were treated to a Jackson-Kippax stand of charm and substance as they added 132 at a crucial stage of the second innings.

The pitch had been deadened by rain, and yet Jack Scott (playing his nineteenth season) and Tim Wall needed watching. Scott erred one over by bowling so wide and short that Jackson ignored the lot, but the tactics might have been deliberate for the batsman showed every sign of 'nibbling', perhaps in his anxiety to keep the scoreboard rolling now that he was through the nervous beginnings. His local followers, spread across the Hill and sitting intently in the Members' Stand, were not at all appreciative of the heart spasms he gave them at regular intervals.

One report of the match grumbled that after an hour's play NSW had made 'only' 51. But though Jackson was in for over an hour and a half before hitting his second four, he kept the singles coming.

The third prong of the attack was Clarrie Grimmett, dropping the ball as if radar-guided onto a teasing spot from a trajectory so flat that even the fleetest-footed batsman was tested almost beyond endurance.

Jackson handled him well throughout – even plundered him once in a while: one soaring off-drive cleared the fence. He played cat and mouse with Vic Richardson's field-setting, drawing the cover men in, driving them out, and piercing the arc with marvellous precision.

The only major hitch in his first innings was an unpleasant blow in the groin from Wall. For some time he hobbled about in agony.

The ground was hushed as he reached 99 in the second innings. Scott hurtled in, bowled, and Jackson turned him for a single that made him the youngest batsman ever to record two separate hundreds in a first-class match.

The 16,000 cheered, whistled and clapped, then filtered home, their day handsomely made. Among them were Archie's mother and father – Mrs Jackson, usually tied to the home, having watched only one cricket match before in her entire life. Their pride was immeasurable long before Archie brought home the silver plate presented by the NSWCA.

When Victoria came to Sydney there were batfuls of runs to be had, but the ironic fact was that Jackson (11 and 44) missed out, Ponsford (6 and 2), perhaps dried up from previous efforts, missed out, Jack Gregory, with whom Jackson opened the NSW innings, missed out, and, in the first innings, so did Bradman. Eight centuries were recorded in front of a record crowd. In this initial season of time-limit matches the batsmen had continued to hold sway.

Archie Jackson, as the match ground its way to a draw, was called upon to bowl and conceded 13 runs in three overs without taking a wicket, an apt return for a ninth-change who, nevertheless, continued to regard himself as a bowler of some potential.

The remainder of the season was swallowed up by a tour of New Zealand with an Australian side composed of some established cricketers and some of the promising youngsters (though Bradman was left at home as a possible replacement). Among the hopefuls were W. C. Alexander and Karl Schneider from SA, and Jackson and McNamee from NSW, but none of them was to reach or remain at the pinnacle of the game for long. Two faded from big cricket and two died young. The first signs of Schneider's fatal illness showed on this tour.

At a mere 5 ft 2 ins easily the smallest first-class cricketer in Australia, this left-hand opening batsman had shown remarkable skill during his youth in Melbourne. Removing to Adelaide, he soon made his mark, even with the handicaps of a short reach and an absence of power in his shots. Patsy Hendren, then coaching in Adelaide and indulging in the fashionable odium of comparisons, saw him as 'the coming Warren Bardsley'.

Schneider made over 500 runs in New Zealand, but towards the end of the tour he collapsed while on picnic with the team on the slopes of Mount Cook.

Several of them were out riding when he suffered a haemorrhage. Among those who carried him back to the hut was Archie Jackson, whose family were never able to erase the query from their minds: was this a dangerous point of contact?

Karl Schneider died – from leukemia – six months later, on September 5, 1928 – Archie Jackson's nineteenth birthday.

The tour had started gaily enough. Jackson and W. C. 'Billy' Bull, the manager, both from the Balmain club, were given a rousing send-off at a dinner at the Dungowan Café. Archie, now a member of the General Committee, though his attendances dropped away steadily over the three seasons he served till his withdrawal in 1930, listened to his skipper, George Wheatley, recall the lad's wonderful 158 against Mosman. Hal Hooker had been swinging the ball two feet that afternoon, but Jackson was master. When he came back into the pavilion it was 'with extreme modesty and the air of having accomplished nothing at all'.

Bull responded for the guests of honour with greater ease than the sweaty-palmed Jackson, who abhorred such occasions, though feeling gratitude at the presentation travelling bag which the club members hoped would serve him through many a tour.

The Australians in New Zealand were unbeaten – in fact untroubled. Woodfull and Ponsford made runs galore, and Grimmett, feted as a returning hero wherever he went in this land of his birth, took 74 wickets, twice as many as Don Blackie, next highest.

Jackson began with 72 against Nelson, 44 against North Otago, and 63 against Otago, then compiled a stylish 110 at Invercargill against Southland, putting on 220 for the first wicket with Bill Ponsford, who also made 110 – a score that worried him because he seemed to make it so often (in his first Test match, too).

The tour was also a social success, though *Smith's Weekly* recorded that Archie was so much in demand, especially by the two daughters of a prominent King's Counsel, that the only ploy guaranteed to overcome his shyness was to invite manager Bull to father's home. The young cricketer invariably accompanied him.

By the time the party reached Gisborne for the eleventh match Archie was mentally and physically weary. In a letter to Bill Hunt he confessed the fact, and also told of a hair-raising incident down in the caves:

> We have been having a great time over here, although I am heartily sick of cricket, and only wish now that we were down at Mt Cook for a good rest. I had a funny experience last week. After we left New Plymouth we spent two hours at the Waitomo Caves, which are

amongst the most beautiful in the world. However, just as we were leaving we decided to go down in the boat and view the glow-worms, which at this time were shining beautifully.

Anyway, as I was getting out I fell in the water amid a hell of a row and got a bit of a ducking. There were quite a number as wet as me, because when I got back into the boat I walked over everyone! But it was certainly funny while it lasted.

Clarrie Grimmett remembered the incident vividly 44 years later: 'Archie was in the bow, and as we approached the landing he tried to pull the boat in, but instead, pushed it away and fell into the black muddy water. Pandemonium broke out as he couldn't swim and we couldn't see him in the darkness. Eventually we got him out, and when we saw him in the light he was absolutely covered in black mud. We took him back to the hotel, washed his clothes, and as we were due to go on to our next town we hung his clothes out of the train windows to dry them and put a rug around him.'

It was a huge joke to Archie, who concluded his letter to Bill Hunt:

I suppose I had better close now as we are going out to a party, but I hope you get among the runs and wickets before the season ends. Hoping to hear from you soon.

Your very sincere pal,
Archie Jackson

Hunt was gradually making his mark as a versatile and aggressive left-arm bowler who played and expostulated in a manner that sometimes provoked opponents – and, in some cases, team-mates. No respecter of persons, Bill trod on toes, laughed infectiously, paid the price occasionally, and would never have changed a minute of it when it came time to look back. From the NSW ranks he was eventually chosen to play for Australia against South Africa at Adelaide in the 1931–32 series. Archie's health had given way by then, and his pleasure and the expressions of congratulation had the edge taken off them by a mutual regret that the Balmain boys were not wearing Australia's colours together.

Bill did the next best thing. He wore Archie's flannels, in spite of an observable tightness. He could never explain quite what made him do it. As it happened, it was his one fond memory of his only Test match. He made 0, took no wickets, and held a solitary catch. Worse, he had a serious difference with the captain, W. M. Woodfull, and a year later he was finding his happiness in the Lancashire League with Rishton.

Archie, able to speak as a very close friend, blamed Bill for the breach: 'I know both of you well enough and I understand both of you. You should have given way, Bill.' It was a simple analysis, and one senses it was near the mark.

For his part, Bill, whose great-heartedness was often masked by a boisterous exuberance, gave his only son two of the most evocative names in cricket: Alan Archie.

The New Zealand tour was wound up with two matches against representative XIs. Jackson, playing in only the first, at Auckland, was caught-and-bowled for 35 by the talented leg-spinner Billy Merritt, and the match was drawn. Woodfull made 284 and featured in two long stands: 184 with Ponsford and 218 with the ill-fated Schneider.

Archie wrote again after that match, and showed his customary concern for his club's affairs:

Balmain seems to have fared very badly, but I heard

that some of you were batting against Jack Gregory in the dark, which I don't suppose is too good a feeling, eh?

Next Saturday the last match of the tour starts, and I will be very pleased indeed when I can say goodbye to my cricket togs for another 6 months anyway.

George Wheatley got out of his trouble all right? Those newspaper reporters make a hell of a row about nothing. They're always the same – always hanging about the dressing-room and when anything happens never forget to put the boot in.

Well, Bill, I suppose I must close now, but I won't be sorry when we're on the *Tahiti* on our way back to Sydney.

Only a few months earlier that same Union Steamship *Tahiti* had been in collision with a ferry in Sydney Harbour. Forty people, including many schoolchildren, were killed. In 1930 the sorry vessel herself sank off New Zealand.

CHAPTER FIVE

GLORY AT ADELAIDE

Percy Chapman's 1928–29 MCC team realised just about as much success as any England side could ever reasonably expect on an Australian tour. Winning four of the Tests and losing one, outclassing the States until the fatigued later stages, and boasting a front rank of Hammond, Hobbs, Sutcliffe, Hendren, Jardine, Larwood, Tate, White and Geary, they were truly what they styled themselves on the Christmas cards they sent home: 'A Happy Family in Australia'.

Australia, for its part, starting with an over-mature side which was soon diminished by the enforced withdrawal of Jack Gregory and Charles Kelleway, could look back at the end of the rubber upon the successful initiation of only two youngsters: Bradman and Jackson. But what youngsters.

The first Test, in which Bradman made his debut, was catastrophic for Australia. Chapman, with a first-innings lead of 399, declined to apply the follow-on and Australia, eventually set 742 for victory, with Gregory and Kelleway unfit, rotted away on a dampened pitch for 66.

Bradman was dropped, but when Ponsford's hand was broken by Larwood in the second Test, which England romped by eight wickets, Bradman found himself reinstated for the third Test, which England won by a

34

much narrower margin. He made 79 and 112, and not only established his place in the side, but became the centrepiece of world cricket for the next twenty years.

It was not until the fourth Test, at Adelaide, that room could be found for Archie Jackson. The public clamour for his selection had been persistent, and as Australia so desperately needed someone to support Woodfull at the opening of the innings, this was the supreme opportunity for inducting the most golden of hopes.

It had to be at the expense of Vic Richardson, whose 82 for South Australia against MCC just before the Test was made off a Larwoodless attack. After learning of his omission Richardson promptly signed up to give the first live Test cricket broadcast from Adelaide Oval.

Richardson's only remaining claim to inclusion – after four batting failures – might have been his sterling fielding. Here Jackson had a curious reputation. His attention still seemed to wander, and the lethargy which observers found excusable and even admirable in his batting brought forth unfavourable comment in the outfield. When moved to it he could swoop on an apparent boundary hit and have it back to the wicketkeeper almost as fast as any. Perhaps it was the poet in him that misted up his concentration.

If he had made a lot of runs in the Test Trial at Melbourne at the start of the season the series might well have run a straighter course for Australia. But he didn't. The only bright performance by an untried player in the Trial was Oxenham's 10 wickets, and it was not until the third Test that *he* was awarded an Australian cap. Jackson had shaped competently, particularly against the testing pace of Gregory. But he did not make enough runs.

He did well for NSW in Brisbane, where they needed 399 to win, and made them comfortably. In the first innings he added 113 with Bradman, who scored a century in each innings, and in the thrilling final assault he and Roy Loder posted 121 for the first wicket.

Then he faced English bowling for the first time – after fielding to a declared total of 734 which was nothing less than a glorious exhibition of masterly English batsmanship. Hammond, who made 225 on this favourite Sydney ground, added a record 333 with Hendren, who was in hard-hitting mood despite (or perhaps because of) a gale-force wind that blew his cap off. As Jardine also made a classic century it was something for the studious youngster to digest.

Maurice Tate beat Jackson with pace and bowled him for only 4, and NSW in due course had to follow on. This time he got a start. Morgan and Andrews were dismissed, but Jackson in company with Kippax seemed able to handle the situation. It was his first taste of Harold Larwood's furious pace, but when he was 40, and the innings was warming, he embarked on a run, misconstruing Kippax's follow-through off a stroke to Freeman, then hesitated. By then Kippax had responded, and would have been stranded. Jackson, never one to shirk obligation, walked past his captain and became the victim of Jardine's underarmed throw. The sacrifice paid handsomely, for Kippax and the next man in, Bradman, saved the match with unbeaten centuries. Both were selected for the first Test.

There was one further chance before the Australian team was chosen and that was several days later when an Australian XI (without any Victorians) played MCC at Sydney. This time Larwood won the first bout, having Jackson caught wide at slip off a weak dab. But in the second innings, again going in at No. 4, he began confidently and batted as his supporters would have wished.

He was graceful, if not commanding. He was never

willing or able to collar an attack brutally, excitedly or arrogantly. To those who enjoyed batting of that kind he never did quite measure up. These were the folk who played Wagner recordings loudly on their wind-up gramophones. Jackson fans preferred something much lighter.

So, having made a noteworthy 61 before glancing a difficult catch to Duckworth, he may well have nurtured private hopes of inclusion in the Test team.

But he had to wait a while yet. It could not be a bad thing for someone only nineteen years old.

A month passed before his next big match. This was the Sheffield Shield contest with Victoria at Melbourne over Christmas, and an historic match it was. Victoria made 376, which seemed more than ample as NSW collapsed to 113 for 9 (Jackson 19 after opening with his hefty friend, Alan 'Noodles' Fairfax).

However, Alan Kippax and Hal Hooker added a hundred runs for the last wicket, and then another hundred, and then yet another, to create a world record which must surely be eternal: 307 for the tenth wicket. Kippax finished 260 not out and Hooker was finally caught for 62.

The New Year match against Queensland found the northern State again a formidable proposition. Cecil Thompson governed affairs with over 200 runs and six wickets, and when Jackson batted a second time, for 53 not out, he had to defend grimly for the sake of his side.

He needed something a little more spectacular than that, and not for the first time South Australia played the Aunt Sally. The setting was Adelaide, and Jackson came within an ace of repeating his feat against them at Sydney the previous season: a century in each innings. Grimmett and Wall provided the obstacles, and the youth in company with his captain danced his way across them all.

His 162 took slightly less than five hours, two of which were spent adding 221 with Kippax.

He sometimes found difficulty in piercing the field, especially when he was on 99. It was galling. Then he tucked the ball away through slips to reach his hundred, and immediately proceeded to go after the bowling, taking another 50 runs in as many minutes. When Fairfax was in obvious bother against Grimmett, Jackson kept him away from the strike until he himself was bowled by the little spinner.

NSW fell away alarmingly in the second innings, and this time Jackson found support in 'Cassie' Andrews, who made 87. Then, with only 10 needed for his second hundred of the match (it would have been his fifth in a row against South Australia), Jackson was caught.

'Jackson for Australia!' went up the cry once more from a public agitated at seeing their Test team now three-down in the 1928–29 series, with two to play. The Ashes were lost, but perhaps there might yet be kindled some hope for the future.

Victoria came to Sydney, and NSW hit 713 for 6 off them. Jackson made 41, Fairfax 104, but the glory belonged to D. G. Bradman, whose 340 not out broke a number of old and revered records. The man had stamina, and he could never be persuaded to agree that he had made enough runs. 'Dainty' Ironmonger knew this, having taken 2 for 220 off 56 overs. Herb Gamble thought so too: he had 2 for 193 off 29 overs. And Hans Ebeling hadn't even a success to cherish in 39 overs.

How they must have envied Hal Hooker who, having made his mark as a No. 11 batsman a month before, polished off the Victoria innings with a hat-trick and took a wicket with his first ball in their follow-on innings.

Victoria passed 500 this time, but the first-innings points

gave NSW the Sheffield Shield for the only time during the proud Archie Jackson's playing career.

By now he was the centre of attention, for the big moment had arrived: he had been invited to play for Australia in the fourth Test, at Adelaide, starting on February 1, 1929. Arthur Mailey scuttled over from the *Sun* newspaper offices and gave the glad tidings to Archie at the shop. Balmain buzzed with joy.

Extraordinarily, England in the last Test played at Adelaide four years previously had lost a high-scoring match by the slender margin of 11 runs, and this time the decision was to be just as razor-thin.

There were several heroes in the match, but three men towered from it: for England, Walter Hammond, who made 119 not out and 177 (following Test scores of 251, 200 and 32), and Jack White, the slow left-arm bowler who appeared such an easy proposition to the distant spectator, and yet, with his coiling wrist action, made the ball dip late in flight and often deviate in to the batsman. Bowling off a short approach, he had by now destroyed all Australian hopes that he would tire sooner or later. In this match he floated down 60 six-ball overs in the first innings and 64.5 in the second, taking 5 for 130 and 8 for 126. ('I used a few shirts and several whisky-and-sodas.')

For Australia the demi-god was the new opening batsman, A. Jackson – soon to be known as A. A. Jackson when he decided to insert his father's name, Alexander, as much in pride as to add uniformity to a scorecard wherein everyone else boasted two initials.

It was very hot as England batted first, and Hobbs and Sutcliffe monumentally raised 143 for the first wicket. Soon, however, the side was in mild difficulties before the spin attack, and it was left to Hammond in one of the toughest innings of his life to carry them to 334. Grimmett bowled craftily, and with due reward took 5 for 102; surprisingly he bowled a wide – a phenomenon in such a parsimonious player.

Then, in mid-afternoon on the Saturday, Woodfull and Jackson went to the middle to answer for Australia. Many were the prayers that the slim youth's first-innings hoodoo would be looking the opposite way this match.

Within minutes the anxiety was directed to the other end: Woodfull was cleverly caught down the leg side by Duckworth for 1; Hendry, on 2, nibbled at Larwood and was also trapped by the keeper; and Kippax was yorked by White, who had been brought on for a couple of overs to enable Larwood and Tate to change ends.

Thus Australia were in a state of shock with three down for 19; the only cheer for the onlookers had come from the unworried manner of 'Boy' Jackson. He drove Tate handsomely and put the full face of the bat to the high pace of Larwood. Whenever Tate pitched on or just outside leg stump Jackson flicked him away through square leg. In this sickening crisis it brought lumps to the throats of the more involved onlookers.

Umpire George Hele, writing later of his close-up view of the Test match newcomer, showed that the crowd was being deluded by the distant, faceless figure standing up to the English onslaught. Archie had leaned forward to his first ball from Tate, who appealed for lbw before noticing that the ball had gone for four. 'This kid'll get a century,' murmured the burly bowler. Umpire Hele recalled the moment of crisis.

I stole a glance at him. An umpire is not supposed to have any feelings, but I was just as keenly interested to see Jackson succeed as any of the 50,000 spectators. It was with something like dismay that I saw Jackson standing there with his face as white as a sheet and nervously trying to moisten his lips. Anybody would have felt sympathetic towards Jackson if they had caught the glimpse I had of him. What a position to be in!

It was not the position for long. The Australian captain, Jack Ryder, came in at No. 5, and his immediate willingness to play shots reminded many that in the Adelaide Test four years ago he had made 201 not out. Now he was driving Larwood with unaccustomed severity. 'Stick to it, son,' he kept saying to Archie between overs. 'You'll be all right, son.'

Jackson saw a ball well pitched up from White, stepped forward, waited for it, and whipped it through the covers to raise the 50. Ryder caught up with him at 30, but he went ahead again and the cheering was tumultuous when he reached his personal 50. The Englishmen were now aware that a rare skill had entered Test cricket, and they too showed their appreciation, wondering, perhaps, what awaited them in the long run, with Bradman already in the high ranks of the Australian force.

It took Ryder and Jackson only one and threequarter hours to add 100 runs after the tense position of Kippax's dismissal. The skipper shortly reached his own 50 – a sound performance, but quite overshadowed by his tousle-haired young partner, physically so far removed from the archetypal Aussie.

At the end of that sweltering day, with a Sunday of rest to follow, Australia were 131 for 3, still 203 behind. But Jackson's polished offering had recharged Australia's interest. Heavy hearts had been lifted.

There had been only one false stroke – an intended glance off Larwood which sent the ball curling up off the edge of the bat short of the 46-year-old Jack Hobbs at cover. Otherwise his poise grew more apparent as the long session wore on (tea was taken between innings, and during this gruelling 160-minute period Geary had to leave the field with a leg injury).

When he reached the sanctuary of the dressing-room Jackson was limp. 'We had to mop him with cold towels,' recalled 'Stork' Hendry many years later, gazing sadly from a wicker chair on his verandah. He spoke his thoughts aloud, as if alone in a meadow: 'Poor little devil.'

Ryder had a tendency to get out early in the morning upon resuming a longish innings, and on the Monday it happened again. He attempted to pull-drive White, who was nagging away still on a perfect length with no-one out for the shot. Ryder was tempted, missed, and adjudged leg-before.

Australia suffered no further losses before lunch, though they needed luck. Bradman looked anything but secure, and Jackson, the talk of the nation now, was tight with tension at the thought of reaching a hundred that would place him in the very select band of those who had made a century in their first England–Australia Test innings. Not only had he the chance of joining that aristocracy, but he would become the youngest member. For today, February 4, 1929, he was just nineteen years and 152 days old.

He had made 97 by lunch, having been unable to do anything constructive with the last four balls. Just previously he had gorgeously late-cut Geary to enter the nineties – a relief after numerous firm drives had been blocked off by White's cover field, Hobbs commanding.

Someone wrote appropriately that throughout that hot morning Jackson had played 'Scotch'.

The two minors, Jackson and Bradman, had weathered a morning of tantalising slow bowling, with Larwood at the other end sometimes bowling to *a concentrated leg-side field of four between fine and square leg.*

They were regarded as bosom pals – the only Australian players staying at the Hotel Richmond, where the England team were quartered. Bradman, who was a year older and currently the youngest Test centurion, discreetly reassured his companion that he need not worry about the hundred. It was sure to come. Just relax.

Jackson, in his turn, addressed himself just as discreetly to umpire Hele during the lunch break, asking if he thought England would take the new ball which was now available. Hele replied that any captain with his head on the right way would take the new ball with his bowlers refreshed.

So, having freshened himself up, Archie Jackson strolled out onto the field of battle again to look for those three precious runs. Larwood, the mightiest fast bowler of them all, reached the end of his long run, turned, and faced the slim lad who was later to christen him, with feeling, 'The Red Devil'. He galloped in, accelerating. The left arm was hoisted high, the right arm screamed round in its full circle, and the new ball, glistening, flashed down on Jackson's off stump. He moved into it and with a clean sweep of the bat steered the ball square and direct to the cover-point fence in front of the Members' Stand before boundary fieldsman Tate could move. Archie was 101, and grinning coyly at the sensation.

The crowd went wild. Hats were tossed in the air. There was a deafening torrent of cheering as they saw their dream come true. The boy had done it! And, launching a festival of thanksgiving, Jackson, when his admirers had finally given up their throaty applause, began to slice the bowling. Duckworth once appealed for leg-before, whooping like a Red Indian, but the cry was turned down, and Duckworth knew the wrath of the crowd, not for the first time.

The timidity that accompanied Jackson through the morning had now vanished, and he applied all his strokes one after the other with nonchalance. He lofted the ball precisely into open spaces, and cut with a delayed wristiness that was pure Macartney. He contrived the swiftest of stolen singles. He glanced the faster balls and drove effortlessly right through the off-side arc so that the tiring bowlers – the three who had done almost all the work, and done it so tidily – must have feared the worst. Larwood padded in over after over, now well under his top pace; White rolled away expressionlessly as if patrolling his Stogumber farm; Tate, whose humour was indestructible, banged the ball into the unresponsive pitch, and eventually had Bradman caught for 40.

They had added 82 in as many minutes, and Mailey commented that it was Bradman's bad luck to have batted with a partner whose brilliancy would have overshadowed any man.

With Ted a'Beckett at the crease, Archie changed his bat and took one or two deep breaths. There were signs of recklessness about him now. When he was 128 he should have been run out, except that Geary's throw was not gathered by Duckworth.

He reached his 150 with a model late-cut for three off Hammond, and then, on 164, he was leg-before trying to turn White. The epic, admired as much by his opponents as by his own people, had ended.

M. A. Noble awarded Jackson the palm for the 'greatest knock of the series' (Hammond's notwithstanding), and the only regret the crowd had was that he had not continued to prosper, particularly as he had just made 51 of 60 with a'Beckett, several times chopping over-pitched balls, with the full face of the bat, with the speed of light past second slip. P. G. H. Fender had only ever seen Macartney do this.

It was over, he was exhausted, he was exhilarated. And tributes to his gallant, near-perfect innings of 164 began to pour in. The SACA presented him with a set of cut glass; some local enthusiasts gave him an inscribed travelling clock, others a rug; at home in Balmain the Mayor called a public meeting to honour him; the Methodist community of Sydney was invited to a gathering at Sydney Town Hall to 'tell him what a credit he is to his country'; a 'bob-in' fund was started in factories and offices.

Archie thought it was all delightful, but he dreaded having to make the necessary speeches; the fearsome prospect of having to rescue Australia's sinking innings was a simple task compared to climbing on a platform to face the listening multitude.

It began that evening, when he received a presentation on the stage of the Garden Theatre. During the day's play he had been escorted to the Vice-Regal box to meet and talk with the State Governor, Sir Alexander Hore-Ruthven.

There was no looking back now. He was an established – not just a promising – national hero, a name in world headlines.

Australia finished with 369, and thus held an unexpected lead of 35. When, on the fourth day, Hobbs and Sutcliffe were out for 21, England's chances rested upon the inexhaustible Hammond and his one reliable defensive partner, Douglas Jardine. They added a record 262, the value of which was revealed when the last eight wickets fell for only 100 runs.

Jackson did not take the field after tea, 12th man Andrews substituting. But while he had patrolled mid-off he had been called upon to stop some smoking-hot drives from Hammond, who was being attacked almost exclusively (and rather puzzlingly) down the off side.

The fifth day was another of sizzling heat: 100 degrees in the shade for much of it. Again Jackson did not field.

Jardine, having negotiated Grimmett's persistent leg-side attack, lost his wicket to Oxenham when two short of a century. Hammond, through sheer tiredness, fell for 177, and it was left to Tate to lift the tail with 47 priceless runs off 50 balls.

Australia needed 349, and the pitch was still innocent. By the fifth evening they had made 24 of them without loss, Woodfull having shielded Jackson from Larwood for most of the session.

On the sixth morning Jackson began edgily, twice snicking White wide of Hammond's right hand. By the time Geary was brought up to strengthen the slips it was too late. The Australian openers progressed well for an hour. Jackson, who had been encouraged by the shrewd old campaigner M. A. Noble to 'come out and go after' slow bowler White, was doing so with fair success – the only Australian for whom this could be claimed. One blow landed the ball on the full on the leg-side pickets, and another sent it swirling over the close field for two. Twice Chapman at silly point intercepted seemingly certain boundary strokes.

Then Woodfull walked down the pitch and had a few words with his young partner, who became subdued. He played two maiden overs from White and then, with his score 36, he was caught behind off Geary. His batting before the issuing of the caution might well have won the match for Australia. As it was, Noble's groan and heated comment were heard all over the Adelaide Press-box. (Umpire George Hele later wrote that Woodfull, far from being critical, was actually saying 'Keep it up, Jacko!')

Woodfull was out soon afterwards, and Hendry fell after lunch. Ryder and Kippax raised Australia's hopes from that point, adding 137 for the fourth wicket against a tiring attack half of which always seemed to be White. Had he broken down there is little doubt that Australia would have cruised to their target.

They came so close. At 308 for 6 (41 needed) they were winning the battle. Then Chapman dived to catch Oxenham, and nerves became strained all round. When Bradman was tragically run out for 58, 29 were still required with two wickets remaining.

Chapman's field setting had come in for criticism. He left the forward short-leg position, through which singles were leaking, open until after lunch – to the fury of the tacticians watching those gripping last minutes.

The match was at boiling point with 23 needed, two wickets left, when lunch was reluctantly taken.

Tate bowled fierily after the break, but it was his catch, taken at the second attempt, from Grimmett that cheered the English camp. By then only 13 were needed.

A fateful 13. For the last wicket fell also at that score. Blackie, already envisaging his popularity should he hit a pair of sixes to save the day, hit White sky-high to leg and Larwood ran like a greyhound to get under it and hugged it as if his future prosperity depended on it.

So England gained a 12-run victory which was all the more sublime for having taken six and a half days of cricket to achieve. Credit was reflected on both sides in an era when Anglo-Australian cricket was at a peak.

Denzil Batchelor, recalling this match in 1950, added another dimension: 'You would have been little understood if you had predicted at Adelaide, 21 years ago, that last year there would be schoolboys writing to ask

Bradman for his autograph, with an urgent postscript "and please sign Sir Don" – schoolboys to whom the very name of the late Archie Jackson meant nothing at all.'

A very young NSW side (which included a promising country lad, Stan McCabe) was selected to play MCC a week later, starting the day after the St Valentine's Day Massacre in faraway Chicago; but the first day was washed out and on the second, when play was agreed at 2.45 pm, only two English players were at the ground. Some had been inspecting the rising framework of the Sydney Harbour Bridge, some went to the races, others had been visiting friends, for they had been told quite positively that there could be no chance of play before 4 o'clock.

The team were hastily gathered up and, with spinner 'Tich' Freeman actually keeping wicket for the first few overs while Ames changed, MCC proceeded to sweep the State side away on a moist wicket for 128, of which Jackson, who was given a loud reception as he walked to the crease, made only 5. Kippax, for the second season running, attained the rare aggregate in Australian first-class cricket of a thousand runs.

Rain washed out the fourth day, and so, with no chance to atone for his inconsiderable failure, Jackson, after a modest performance against his old favourites South Australia, went to Melbourne for the final Test of the 1928–29 series.

It was the turn of the tide for Australia, who introduced three young players – Tim Wall, Percy Hornibrook and Alan Fairfax. England lacked her captain, Chapman, who had influenza, and Sutcliffe, who had a shoulder strain. Their places were taken by Ernest Tyldesley and Maurice Leyland, the latter, in this eight-day match, the longest ever between England and Australia, scoring 137 in his first Ashes Test innings.

Above: A Glasgow studio photo of Archie Jackson, aged about one year, with his mother.

Soon to be the keenest little cricketer in Ferdinand Street, Balmain, Archie is snapped outside the family home at No. 14. The first-floor balcony once almost cost him his young life.

Solemn-faced Test cricketer of the future (*centre*): Archie Jackson at primary school –
the remains of a crumbling photograph.

The other love: football. Archie (*front, left*) with a school team, short of sartorial
elegance but with a full endowment of enthusiasm.

The Birchgrove school cricket team, smartly attired. Archie Jackson, captain, is seated left of the trophy.

Birchgrove Oval, scene of rapturous boyhood hours and of many of Jackson's artistic grade innings as well as the lonely dedication of early morning practice.

Four 'cracks' of Rozelle, pictured in the local paper, December 1923: Dudley Seddon, Bill Hunt, Archie Jackson and Syd Hird, all first-class cricketers of the near future. No school stood a chance against them. Jackson averaged 79, Seddon 78; Hunt took 43 wickets at 3, Hird 64 at 4.

Aged 17, now rather more than a twiglet of a batsman: sleeves just clear of the wrists, slatted pads, an easy swing of the bat.

The ease of style is apparent even from a distance. Jackson, opening the NSW innings with Jack Gregory against Victoria at Sydney in 1927–28, plays Morton back down the pitch. This time the teenage batsman missed out, though a record eight centuries were scored in the match, four in this innings.

The Australian combination which went undefeated through New Zealand in 1927–28. Standing: Bert Oldfield, Ray McNamee, Frank Morton, W. C. Bull (manager), Don Blackie, Archie Jackson, Karl Schneider; seated: Bill Ponsford, Bill Woodfull, Vic Richardson (captain), Alan Kippax, Clarrie Grimmett.

Capped by Australia: Archie Jackson, photographed by England's greatest batsman, Jack Hobbs.

How Archie loved net practice – always a sure pointer to the truest love of the game.

White won the toss, but England were laborious on the first day, the highlight of which was Jack Hobbs's twelfth and final century against Australia. They batted all through the second day as well, Leyland making his hundred and several of the Australians running (or slipping) into criticism for being poorly 'spiked'. Jackson was one who went sprawling as he attempted to scoop up a ball on the boundary, and the offence was seen to be much more serious when he finally had the chance to bat.

England totalled 519, and Woodfull and Jackson opened cautiously against Larwood and Tate. After 54 balls only two runs had come. Then the pace increased, and the score had mounted to 54 in an hour and a half when Jackson (30) slipped in starting out for a single to Larwood deep at point. The fast bowler's return to Geary was swift, and another pretty Jackson innings was over.

Woodfull went on to make a century, as did Bradman, and Australia were not too far behind after all. But the runs were hard-won and the daily output was proving tiresome to a public that was probably getting too much Test cricket.

England made 257 the second time, which left Australia to make 286. They started half an hour from the end of the sixth day, Oldfield and Hornibrook the 'nightwatchmen' openers. They survived, through several near misses, until lunch-time on the seventh day, by which time 51 of the runs had been made. When the plucky Oldfield left at 80, Jackson joined Woodfull, and they saw the score to 129 after tea, at which point the captain was bowled – for the first time in 27 months of first-class cricket. Hammond worked the trick (though it was 'played on' and not 'clean bowled'), and began to make the ball kick sharply. One spiteful delivery hit Jackson in the chest; another hit wicketkeeper Duckworth in the neck. It gave England real hope of achieving a five-nil whitewash.

For a time, with Kippax as his partner, Jackson post-poned that hope with a series of lovely drives square and straight. But a marvellous delivery from Geary bowled him for 46 (leaving him eight short of a thousand for the season), and the fieldsmen became more sprightly as the bowlers pressed for victory. At the end of the seventh day Australia needed 113 to win with six wickets standing.

When Kippax was run out going for a fourth run next morning the game was evenly poised still: 82 to win, five men to fall. Bradman joined Ryder, and ought to have been stumped; but the most decisive incident was when Ryder received a dubious benefit from the umpire after Leyland had thrown the wicket down from mid-on.

Shortly after lunch the runs were made without further loss. For Australia the taste of victory was good. Self-respect had returned. Now it seemed that the advent of Jackson, Bradman, Fairfax, Oxenham, and Wall would stand Australia in good stead for years to come, and the perennial sadness at the termination of another Test series was matched by the expectation of a very special return rubber in England in a year's time.

As a footnote to the match, the most extraordinary spec-tacle occurred after the victory when, in the chaos of the celebration, no car could be found to take the four NSW players to catch their train to Sydney. In the emergency they commandeered a horse-drawn cab, which presented an odd sight as it clopped along with Messrs Kippax, Fairfax, Bradman and Jackson squeezed inside the cabin and perched on the step and dicky-seat.

It must have reminded the grinning Jackson of the Balmain laundry cart.

CHAPTER SIX

FROST ON THE BLOOM

The Jacksons were deeply proud of their boy, and let it be known to the queue of reporters who called at Ferdinand Street for a 'domestic angle'. His mother recalled childhood incidents which, in reality, had not taken place so very long ago. Sister Lil spoke of the tussles she had had with her brother: she, being the strongest and highest-spirited of the girls, used to take him on whenever he was in a romping mood.

'Always fighting,' said mother. 'We all knew he would make good at cricket ... There's not a quieter, more modest boy in Sydney ... We have to drag the words out of him ... he won't repeat things unless he's pressed ... Archie never boasts....' Then she whispered reflectively: 'We won't say that he wasn't disappointed a little at the beginning of the season.'

One interviewer who had managed to talk to him direct came away with the impression that 'force of character is latent in him. There is no sign of aggression in his demeanour, a characteristic which has not a little to do with his popularity.'

At Balmain Town Hall on May 11 he was presented with an inscribed silver tea service and a cheque for £200, the proceeds of the Testimonial. It was a gala evening, with stage skits which alluded almost monotonously to the hero of the hour. The Mayor made the presentation after a number of speeches during which one alderman reminded the citizens that Balmain, as well as being the birthplace of F. R. Spofforth, had also seen much of another early Australian cricket champion, W. L. Murdoch.

M. A. Noble paid his tribute and Dr L. O. S. Poidevin indulged in a play on names by referring to another great Archie (MacLaren) and another great Jackson (Hon. F. S.), both fine English cricketers whose combined batting and captaincy achievements he hoped Balmain's Archie might one day emulate.

The Rev. Sam McKibbin, the local Methodist minister and a younger brother of Tom, the former Australian Test bowler, recounted his pride at having bowled Archie out years ago. Alan Kippax, more seriously, predicted that at the end of the 1930 tour of England Archie would be clearly the best batsman in the world.

When Archie stood to respond, the cheering lasted some time, which could not have allayed his nervousness. But he maintained his composure and in a neat little speech he thanked his admirers and friends for all they had done for him, and expressed the hope that he would be associated with Balmain for many years to come.

The speech reduced him, but after the Mayor's wife had presented Mrs Jackson with a basket of flowers he came to his mother's rescue, responding on her behalf.

His popularity at times became a trial both to Archie and the family. Callers arrived at all hours, and though he was sometimes driven to asking Mum to tell them he was out, the blue De Soto sedan of which he was now the unashamedly proud owner stood in the street as an advertisement that the star was at home.

He often brought his pals in for a feed, and to some he

became very attached. Arthur Allsopp, a hard-hitting batsman whose promise was never quite fulfilled, was a special friend. He was staying with the Jacksons one weekend when a cricket banquet was being held in the city, and because Allsopp had no formal clothes, Archie, who by now had the necessary dress for such occasions, refused to go either. The problem was overcome by adapting Mr Jackson's navy pinstripe suit, blackening Allsopp's brown shoes, and pinning on a makeshift bow-tie. (The only real vanity observed in Archie was a muttered dread of baldness; in clothes he preferred casual styles.)

On a less happy occasion another 'friend' stayed at the house overnight, and when Archie paid a visit next day to the dentist (Australian Test batsman Johnny Taylor) he discovered that his trouser pockets had been cleared out.

Such money as came his way he did not squander. He knew the value of a shilling after the deprivations of past years. And as the Great Depression later bit into the economy and his father's earnings dropped he pledged himself never to allow his mother to go to work.

He played only five first-class matches and had only five innings for Balmain the following season, 1929–30, when ill-health began to stalk him. He was hugely successful in all bar one of the major fixtures, and was never other than an automatic choice for the England tour.

He began with an 80 at Brisbane, and two centuries of varying significance at Sydney. The first was an attractive 168 not out against A. H. H. Gilligan's MCC team on their way to New Zealand. Though he made the runs off a depleted attack he treated the veteran Frank Woolley's slow left-arm bowling with less respect than was decent, and stood up well to the fast deliveries of Maurice Allom, who was to take four wickets in five balls a few weeks later in a Test match at Christchurch. His hundred came in a mere two and a quarter hours when he pulled a no-ball from Woolley for four. Against loose bowling he scored thereafter at a run a minute till the declaration.

It was a high-scoring match: Bradman, Kippax and Allsopp (in his first first-class innings) all made centuries, and the budding champion McCabe hit 90; and for MCC, Maurice Turnbull made 100 and Woolley 219. So bizarre was the final innings of this drawn match that Jackson was called upon to bowl four overs, which realised 28 runs.

But it was in the next match, billed as a Test Trial, that he played the classic innings of the season – some said of his lifetime. The sides – Ryder's XI and Woodfull's XI – contained, for the first time ever, players from all six States of the Commonwealth. Jackson was among those who must have felt that they were not exactly on trial; at least, he opened the match with remarkable confidence, driving everything up to him with a freedom that amounted almost to indifference.

The day was warm, and five thousand people were present when Wall stormed in from the Paddington end to start proceedings. Boundaries were soon coming with regularity from Jackson, but Ponsford was watchful. The only hitch came when Fairfax hit Jackson on the left knee, dashing to his aid as he lurched around in agony. Soon he was hitting Blackie through long-off then loftily to the long-on boundary. In due course a slashing hit off the same bowler brought up the hundred and at lunch, after 100 minutes' play, the total was 122: Jackson 81, Ponsford 41 (including a boundary shot that uprooted a picket from the fence).

In the afternoon Jackson again powerfully drove the cunning Blackie, and it was remarked that seldom had he driven with such gusto. He reached 99, and stroked Blackie straight, but the bowler intercepted. Two balls later he thrust him through point for another boundary, his fifteenth, and the glorious century was his.

Nor did he wilt there. The Tasmanian, Burrows, was called into the attack, and Jackson took 15 off his first over, one straight-drive whistling through the bowler's desperate fingers. Blackie continued to suffer as he had never suffered before. Jackson hit him mercilessly, going down on one knee and swinging him to the leg fence.

Ponsford began to pepper the field too, and the score moved from 150 to 200 in twenty minutes. The crowd had built up to ten thousand by then, and pleased they were to see Jackson hoist the steady Hornibrook for a straight six. A single off Wall, who was still occasionally getting the ball to kick head-high, made him 150.

His pal Fairfax came on at the Randwick end, and he grinned mischievously as he cut him twice for fours to reach 170, his highest in first-class cricket. Off the seventh ball he square-drove another flashing four. Where would it end? No bowler could logically hope to defeat him this day. Ponsford, the record-breaker, was batting exceptionally well, but he was dwarfed by Jackson's magnificence.

Eventually he swung carelessly at Hornibrook and missed, then skyed the next to cover, where Kippax took the catch. The stand of 278 had lasted 187 minutes, and Jackson's 182 included 27 fours and a six. Again a long hyperactive innings had taken much out of him.

After Archie's memorable 182 in the Test Trial at Sydney, the score continued to mount, reaching 663. Woodfull's team were then shot out by Oxenham and Grimmett for 309 and followed on; but Bradman added a double-century to his first-innings century, and Kippax stroked 170 in celebration at having overthrown a recent illness, and Ryder's side went in needing 188.

This time Jackson was kept back to No. 7 and the 'youngsters' batted ahead of him. Trouble lay ahead: Hornibrook and Blackie wove their spell on a rain-damaged pitch, McCabe was easily top-scorer with 46, Jackson was caught behind for 15, and it was left to Ryder and Grimmett to scrape the winning runs with nine down.

It may well have been during this match that Archie Jackson's grey-blue eyes fell upon a crippled boy who sat watching other lads playing cricket on the expanse of Moore Park. The boy explained that on account of his handicap he was not allowed to play.

'Will you be here tomorrow?' Archie asked him, and the next morning he brought an autographed bat along for him and played with him till it was time to prepare for the big match. Understandably the gesture was never forgotten.

Just before Christmas NSW had a reversal at Adelaide. South Australia amassed 508 and Clarrie Grimmett did the rest; but the newcomers, McCabe and Allsopp, both made runs in both innings, and a further bright spot was the opening partnership between Bradman and Jackson in the second innings. Facing arrears of 194, they placed 172 on the board before Bradman was leg-before to Grimmett. He had taken an unsavoury knock in the stomach from Wall early in the innings, but this did not upset his plan of stepping out to Grimmett when most batsmen were driven back.

Jackson, neat and unruffled as ever, once swung Grimmett full-toss into the stand for six and showed during his 82 that he was in every sense a master batsman. Bradman, for all his efficiency, was recognised as having a 'resource' that 'made up for what he lacked in grace'.

His alleged lack of grace was almost beside the point early in the New Year as he compiled a new world-record

score of 452 not out at Sydney against Queensland. To
anyone who might have overlooked the fact, D. G.
Bradman was positively and irrevocably a world name –
a maker rather than a gatherer of runs, always 'a better
batsman than the other fellow is a bowler', never satisfied
with a century or even a double-century so long as his
team occupied the crease. Some Englishmen may have
been sceptical of the angle of his bat, but it usually came
down straight, usually met the ball centrally, and usually
was raised aloft every hour or so to acknowledge the
applause for another 50 runs.

The national selectors had not to think about his name
or several others when they drew up their list for England.
It was simply a matter of filling the last five or six
places.

Archie Jackson missed the Victoria match at Melbourne
and Bradman's Queensland match, besides the home
match with South Australia. The vicious seed of tuberculosis
was in him, though it was not fully understood.
He had been forced into hospital in Adelaide after the
Christmas match there, and the authorities began to feel
concern for him.

He returned for the Victoria match at Sydney, but
made only 5 in a rain-ruined interlude that forced the
selectors to postpone their final choice for England.

Soon, however, the names were announced amid the
seasonal jubilation and heartbreak: W. M. Woodfull
(captain), V. Y. Richardson (vice-captain), A. F. Kippax,
D. G. Bradman, A. Jackson, S. J. McCabe, A. G. Fairfax,
W. A. Oldfield, W. H. Ponsford, E. L. a'Beckett, C. V.
Grimmett, T. W. Wall, C.W. Walker, P. M. Hornibrook,
and A. Hurwood.

Balmain responded with another 'bob-in' appeal which
raised for their hero £212, a hundred of which was handed

to Mrs Jackson by her grateful son as contribution towards a new house in Drummoyne. (Dad, true to form, had put in his shilling without comment when a collector approached him, not knowing who he was.) And at a Balmain 'smoko' at the Town Hall, Archie was presented with a cabin wardrobe.

The Board of Control, as one of its main preparatory tasks, arranged for Jackson to have his tonsils removed. Ponsford had suffered from tonsillitis on the previous tour, and it seems the Board was anxious to prevent a similar occurrence. But the Jackson family always regarded the operation as having been needless. Archie had never been troubled by his tonsils. Indeed his only remembered sicknesses had been childhood ailments, such as mumps, measles, chickenpox.

Dr Reg Bettington, who played cricket for NSW and Middlesex and was a triple Blue at Oxford, was in practice as an ear, nose and throat specialist at Manly, and it was he who performed the surgery. It affected Jackson adversely, as the family recall. He lost a stone in weight, and became even more poorly after catching a chill in Tasmania, where the team played two matches.

But it was a leisured age, and the team, after crossing Australia by train and playing against Western Australia, travelled by ship – not aircraft – to Britain. This allowed the cricketers to get to know each other and helped assuage the wear and tear of the past season.

It also gave Archie the opportunity to win the peg quoits competition, much to his own amusement. It was fun and games the whole way, with an off-beat episode in Ceylon when the team, wearing topees, played a Colombo side. Rain, that seemed to follow them across the world, cut short this match.

They disembarked at Naples and crammed in a lot of

European sightseeing before confronting the sublime vision of Dover's white cliffs. Australians of that era used to refer to this as 'reaching Home'.

CHAPTER SEVEN

ENGLAND, 1930

'If the Australian team has no Macartney it will at least have Archie Jackson,' promised the *Mail*, whose observer went on to say that Bradman and Jackson, to judge from their fresh, smooth faces, might both have been undergraduates instead of tempered heroes of a score of classic innings against some of the best bowling in the world.

The *Sydney Mail* had already lodged a large claim on Jackson's behalf: 'On Australian wickets, and judged solely on stroke technique, Archie Jackson may be justifiably regarded as the greatest of present-day batsmen – greater even than Walter Hammond.... He was not forced, as was Hammond repeatedly, to look for runs in one direction.'

His reputation travelled well ahead of him, and all eyes were on him at the preliminary net practices at Lord's.

Indeed, all eyes had been on him when *Orford* landed the team at Dover, as were those of a woman correspondent who quoted him as being against cricketers' wives touring with them. 'When we're not playing,' he told her, 'I just want to go round London by myself. I love London. I saw the rain the day we arrived and the sun yesterday and today, and I like them both.'

She had a scoop, for the *Daily Chronicle* man had ruefully to report that 'a younger and handsomer lot have never before come in quest of the Ashes – nor one more silent. . . . Silence with them, however, is both legal and compulsory. Each man carries a formidable legal document.'

Lord Harris, who had led England against Australia before any of the team was born, welcomed them as they disembarked – eleven of the fifteen stepping onto English soil for the first time (assuming the infant Jackson had never been taken south of the border). They faced a battery of cameras and questions, and most of the crowd seemed astounded at their overall youthfulness.

'These bronzed, keen-eyed, spare athletes are for the greater part a team of boys. If you put players like McCabe, Jackson, Bradman and Walker in school caps they would be almost like the enthusiastic boys who will hunt them all summer in search of forbidden autographs.'

Autographs were indeed banned, at least at Lord's.

A huge crowd had been building up outside Victoria Station for over an hour to greet them as the boat-train arrived. As Vic Richardson recalled in his autobiography, when Australia's Prime Minister Scullin arrived in London later that summer it was, in contrast, days before his presence was public knowledge.

They stayed at the Midland Grand Hotel, St Pancras, and the first offical engagement was the High Commissioner's welcome at Australia House. When Sir Granville Ryrie had finished with them they went on to the Savoy Hotel for a reception by the British Sportsman's Club, with the Duke of Gloucester present. King George V's message of greeting was read out, Lord Harris toasted them, Woodfull responded, then they continued on to Lord's for a light work-out in the fresh spring air.

The big occasions mounted up: the laying of a wreath at St Clement Dane's Church on Anzac Day (with Jackson, Bradman and Fairfax going on to the National Liberal

Club for dinner and billiards), a formal Gala Performance in their honour at the Coliseum (with Archie Jackson looking even younger in a dinner jacket than in flannels), and – the greatest of thrills for him – seats just behind the King's box at Wembley for the FA Cup final between Huddersfield Town and Arsenal, when the Graf Zeppelin put in an eerie appearance over the packed stadium.

The net practices continued as reminders of the purpose of their tour, and the forecasts and analyses proliferated.

The *Evening News* spy saw Bradman, in his bright blue NSW cap, make a 'few preliminary flourishes', then Jackson unwittingly lured the entire audience to himself. All the MCC ground-staff boys gathered round, and 'Plum' Warner escorted his young son across to see the wonder from Australia.

Jackson gave them all the strokes: the swish off the toes, the late-cut, and the square-drive which everyone seemed to have heard about. Then Grimmett spun a couple of googlies through him and grinned. Jackson nodded his appreciation.

'He looks,' noted the *News* correspondent, 'like any English public school boy, is quiet, and a little shy. There is something of the Hobbs about Jackson, the stylist.'

Geoffrey Tebbutt, who covered the tour for Australian Press Association, put it this way: 'The English, who worship style in horses, dogs, evening clothes, and batting, got ready to acclaim young Jackson.'

Somerset's M. D. Lyon, another keen observer, wrote in the *Daily Sketch*: 'Jackson looked about the best batsman to me. He is a little on the short side, but obviously strong and supple.'

Supple he always was; but his strength was fast becoming an illusion.

Things went wrong from the start. Bouts of illness were

so considerable that he even missed some enticing social functions. And he was generally uneasy on the damp, greenish pitches. It has become a familiar problem: the look and feel of English wickets in April and May can so easily instil an unreasoning apprehension into the mind of a young visiting batsman.

No such phobia troubled Don Bradman, who had an utterly sensational tour, having built for himself the advantage of a roaring start (236, 185, 78) free of the misfortune of being caught miraculously at the start of an innings.

Jackson's first innings, against Worcestershire, ended in such a way. He had been far from certain, especially against Fred Root's in-duckers; but, swinging hard at a poor-length ball from Brook, he was mortified to see Cyril Walters conjure a catch at forward short leg.

He failed at Leicester, though Jack Hobbs wrote of him flatteringly, and batting No. 5 against Essex at Leyton in bitterly cold weather he made some charming strokes in the second innings before being caught off his 'chop shot'.

In glimpses he was showing the English public a sample of his culture; but he was not making centuries, or even half-centuries.

There came a happy interlude when he met his cousin James in Liverpool. Their fathers were brothers, and James's sire had returned with Sandy from Australia the first time and remained in Scotland. For years there had been no contact, but James, who captained Liverpool Football Club, had taken it upon himself while laid up with a knee injury to enquire if this young Australian cricketer could possibly be his cousin. He was, and he was granted a day's leave to visit.

While in Liverpool several of the players tried unsuccessfully to telephone relatives in Sydney, but they had more luck a week later in London, Jackson and Fairfax speaking to relatives, friends and club-mates and hearing them quite clearly in return.

Off Lancashire Jackson made a pleasant 40, hooking well, and drawing a further expert opinion on his style, this time from the irrepressible Cecil Parkin: 'He is perhaps a little slow – a Conservative at the crease. But he may become a batting Bolshevik any time. It is my opinion that he is a better bat than Bradman.'

The team returned to London for the MCC match – Archie's first appearance at Lord's. In front of a capacity house he made a duck, caught behind off Allom.

In the second innings he was criticised for poor running and backing up, and was even blamed for Woodfull's downfall, the skipper tumbling over after being sent back and, with his arm hurt, playing on shortly afterwards.

But Jackson managed his first fifty of the tour, reached with a sweetly on-driven six off G. T. S. Stevens, and went on to a carefully-made 64 before Hendren picked him up wonderfully at slip.

Still there was dissatisfaction and disappointment. C. G. Macartney, who was covering the tour for the *Mirror*, was concerned at the absence of freedom in his strokeplay. And though there had been universal pleasure after lunch when he 'almost revealed his old self' he still seemed cramped much of the time.

It was looking better for him in the near-freezing conditions at Chesterfield, where he and Ponsford opened with 127. He was all at sea against Tommy Mitchell's leg-breaks, but weathered the spell and actually on-drove him on the full for six. Later he landed Townsend into the pavilion. But he failed against Surrey, 'hanging his bat out ingloriously', and followed that with nought against Hampshire in the match in which, in pouring rain, Bradman achieved his thousand runs by the end of May.

Then came Lord's again, the Middlesex match, when he showed truer touch without making many runs and came in for some barracking during a tedious period. Percy Hornibrook remembered his saying 'Be damned – I'll show them'. And he refused to make a shot for several overs.

At least, as Bradman and Jackson shared a modest stand 'Plum' Warner was moved to see them as 'names destined to appear on the scoresheet for many a long year.'

What bliss there is in our blindness to events yet un-revealed.

During the Cambridge University match the players were invited to Sandringham Castle to meet the King and Queen, but Archie had been unwell again and had to miss what for some was the highlight of the summer. He did not complain.

By now the first Test was imminent, and Arthur Mailey made a poignant plea in the *Daily Herald* for his protégé's selection, urging it if for no other reason than that his great ability was now undoubted: 'Jackson is a match-winner, and I am sure he will yet thrill and surprise the English cricket public by his artistry and technique.'

But with most of the batsmen in fair form there was no real case for including a man so much out of touch that he was seen halfway back on his right leg before the bowler's arm was over.

The Australians conditioned themselves for the first Test by withdrawing in secrecy to Downside School, and it was there that a reporter peeped through the hedge and saw Jackson and Wall playing a vigorous game of tennis. For Wall, who was in the team, it served as a distracting loosener. For Jackson, 12th man, it offered a chance to let off steam.

England won the Test by 93 runs, but it was to be the

only defeat suffered by the Australians throughout the tour.

The baggage was all shifted back to London for the Surrey match, and by now two bags stood out conspicuously. They belonged to Kippax and Jackson (obviously from the sports shop) and were each adorned with four handles and painted yellow and green all over. 'Seemingly big enough to accommodate a kangaroo,' thought one gaping onlooker.

It was reported at this time that Jackson's illness had at first been thought serious, but he was now back in the side, making 37 not out, driving well, and looking more like the batsman of the previous season.

He made 52 against Lancashire, late-cutting often and having some overdue luck. Hodgson, who struck him in the chest early in the innings, finally knocked his off stump back.

He had not done enough to find a place in the second Test, at Lord's, though he went to Blackpool beforehand to 'tone up' with some members of the team and a group of the Lancashire players. Other diversions included golf at the West Kent course, and mini-cricket with a Woolworths bat and golf ball on the lawn of friends at Bickley.

The Lord's Test match was a classic, made even more memorable by the sight of the R101 airship as it loomed overhead – an ill-starred giant that was to crash to its death the day the Australians sailed for home.

Duleepsinhji and Chapman made centuries for England, but 155 by Woodfull and a perfect 254 by Bradman ensured an eventual seven-wicket victory for Australia that levelled the series. Archie nearly played when Bradman was late to arrive on the opening morning. He was getting changed as The Don hurried up the stairs.

Jackson now uncovered better form. In the acid test of

the Yorkshire match at Bradford his 46 contained some scintillating strokes, and though he made only a third of the runs in a stand of 138 with Ponsford, hopes were rising.

Next came Notts, and scores of 22 and 79. But the most significant events were Fairfax's admission to hospital for an operation and Ponsford's sudden attack of gastritis. This left the vacancy which Jackson might have forced in any case. He was chosen for the third Test, at Leeds, which pleased, among many, Neville Cardus, then writing as 'Cricketer' in the *Manchester Guardian*. He had been fascinated by Archie Jackson at Old Trafford: 'Somehow Jackson gave us a flavour. He is an enigma on English cricket fields, so far. You can feel intuitively that he is a cultured batsman; every now and again he lets us see a stroke that none but the elect can ever hope to perform. Checked action, born of no confidence, is at present hindering the gush of his quality. Woodfull ought to keep him in the XI until class has come forth, as sooner or later class will.'

Recalling the best of Australian batsmen – Trumper, Hill, Macartney, Gregory, Ransford, Darling – he reminded readers and players alike that 'the scoreboard was not *their* eternal looking-glass.'

Archie Jackson's part in the third Test match was soon over. Opening with his captain, he made but one run before being caught at short leg by Larwood off Tate. Bradman replaced him and finished with 334; Kippax made 77; Australia amassed 566; and a painstaking century by Hammond (together with rain and bad-light stoppages) deprived Australia of victory.

Jackson was also deprived of a second innings by England's follow-on just when those with active memories were wondering what devilish punishment he might unleash – as he had so often second time round. His only further chance to distinguish himself was when Tate lofted Grimmett to long-on: the catch was safely pouched.

Trevor Wignall of the *Daily Express* had seen him at the Queens Hotel just after breakfast on the first morning of the match, and could not help noticing his tenseness. He attributed Archie's failure more to anxiety than anything else.

Wignall saw much of him off the field, and was impressed by his gentleness and sincerity as much as by his absentmindedness. Not only did he frequently mislay his batting-gloves or his shirt, but he even overlooked an official invitation to luncheon at the House of Commons – an oversight that upset him when it was pointed out.

By the end of the tour Wignall was certain that Archie's nervous little cough had grown appreciably in strength.

From Leeds they visited Scotland for two matches in a misty and damp July. In the first, at Edinburgh, Jackson did not bat, but at Glasgow, in a match against a Scottish XI, he spent over two hours batting on his native turf, compiling a 52 not out that gave him a special satisfaction.

The following day he wrote to Bill Hunt from the Palatine Hotel in Sunderland, the handwriting even and elegant as ever, the mood unquenchably cheerful:

We are having a splendid time over here and I would like to stay on for a few months after our tour ends. Today we are scheduled to play Durham but it has rained so heavily that the match was abandoned. We have just concluded our trip to Scotland and everyone had a marvellous time. Of course I had some relatives there and had to look them up. They were living at Gourock, a small village twenty miles from Glasgow on the River Clyde, and we had a wonderful view of many famous Lochs and beauty spots such as Dunoon, where Harry Lauder resides, Rothesay, Loch Long, and Loch Lomond.

Scotland is indeed a beautiful country, and I intend to spend a week there in September. I expect to see some of the big soccer matches, so that I am staying in Liverpool with my cousin James, who captains the Liverpool team. The two matches I shall see will be against Blackburn Rovers and Huddersfield Town.

Last month I paid a visit to Wimbledon and saw the world's best tennis players in action, viz Tilden, Cochet, Borotra, Crawford, Helen Wills, Miss Ryan, etc. I consider Tilden to be the best of them all. He is a great player indeed.

We have been playing quite a lot of tennis and golf lately. It is, after all, a spell from cricket, isn't it? And one needs a rest from the mental side of the game. I am doing better now with the bat than when we first arrived in England, and have now scored 650 runs at an average of 35.00 so that if I can maintain my form or exceed it I should total between 1300 and 1400 runs.

He then congratulated Bill on doing well for Balmain, expressing the hope that he would get in the NSW team in the new season, and extended best wishes to him and his fiancée Ann.

There was no great dissatisfaction or frustration in this private letter, which might have served as a ready medium for someone needing to pour out the bitterness, the exasperation, the excuses.

Could it be that he was not really all that concerned? The laboured innings seem to discount that conjecture. There seems but one conclusion: he kept it all inside him. He would not have been the first nor the last touring cricketer to sob a little in the solitude of a hotel room.

'What does it matter, as long as we win?' Archie remarked to Bradman after learning of his exclusion from the fourth Test, at Old Trafford.

But he missed very little. Rain and poor light cut hours from the match, and neither side batted twice.

It was a relief to move on to the West Country, the more so when Jackson and Bradman joined forces to pulverise the Somerset bowling. They added 231 runs, and at last – at long last – Archie Jackson reached a hundred. The Taunton sun, it was said, had thawed him out!

He owed a lot to Arthur Wellard for dropping him early, but no-one could dispute that his luck was overdue. The first half of his innings was as tame and laboured as the second half was spirited. He was in for four hours and finished with 118, with fifteen fours, several off his 1928–29 'enemy' Jack White. It was a very popular success.

Perhaps he was lifted by a 'good luck' cable from home, inspired by Dr Evatt, who urged at the annual meeting of the Balmain club that a vote of confidence be rendered. In his speech he had offered the theory that the continual changing from opener to middle-order batsman had upset Jackson's approach.

He made a few runs against Glamorgan on the brand new pitch at St Helens, and at Northampton when the Australians followed on he compiled a lovely 52, though having twisted an ankle in trying to save a boundary.

By now he had worked his way back into the Test side for the final encounter, at The Oval. It was to be his last Test match against England.

He took Vic Richardson's place (one report stated that it was at Richardson's own suggestion) as he had done at Adelaide for his first Test match. But the more surprising changes were in the England side, where 42-year-old Whysall came in as an extra batsman, Gloucestershire's penetrative off-spinner Goddard was omitted, and there was a change of captaincy: Percy Chapman, whose effervescent leadership had taken England to six successive victories over Australia from 1926 to 1930, was viewed by the selectors as being too volatile and flamboyant for what was likely to be a grim decider (his hard line at Brisbane in 1928 seemed forgotten).

Bob Wyatt took over, and received at least one threat on his life for his – or the selectors' – temerity.

It was Wyatt's partnership with the cool, determined Sutcliffe (161) that salvaged England's innings. The captain came in at 197 for 5 and weathered a nerve-tingling period, the stand of 170 enabling England to go on past 400 before Grimmett wrapped up the innings.

Jackson had distinguished himself so far with fine ground-fielding and throwing, and by hurtling head-first into the crowd after chasing a boundary hit. There were gasps all round, but no serious injury, and the spectators concerned were left 'proudly displaying the bruises they earned in the great match'.

Australia replied forcefully, reaching 159 without loss by tea on the second day, after which Ponsford's unlucky 110 (made in only two and a quarter hours) once again proved his downfall. In the gloom and after having been taken ill at the adjournment, he was bowled by leg-spinner Peebles, another Scottish-born cricketer; now Bradman came out, having made 742 runs already in six Test innings that summer.

A shower drove the players in immediately, but they soon returned – this time for the batsmen to appeal against the dullness. They were off for half an hour, and soon after resumption Peebles had Woodfull caught behind. That made it 190 for 2 – evenly poised as Kippax joined Bradman.

England pressed, but could make no further headway on a pitch that was offering little to the bowlers. At the end of the third day Australia were 215 for 2, still 190 behind.

Runs came steadily on the Tuesday, even when Larwood and Tate used the new ball. Peebles struck again, this time having Kippax nicely caught by Wyatt at short leg for 28: 263 for 3.

Jackson negotiated the steps and strode out across the grass, arguing with his nerves the whole way. He and Bradman, a pair who in tandem had made so many runs over the past two years, now faced a critical situation. The runs had to be made in this first innings, for the pitch was fully expected to turn in the later stages.

Peebles bowled, and Jackson drove him wide of mid-off and scampered off for his first run: Hobbs swooped across from cover, picked up the ball and in one movement underarmed it at the bowler's stumps with Jackson still yards from home. Peebles had no chance of getting back to gather it, so swift had been the interception, and the ball bounced past its target. Lucky Jackson even had time to run an overthrow as he ruminated on the death he had escaped.

Ian Peebles was bowling beautifully. A perfect-length googly beat Jackson, and the leg stump, and keeper Duckworth, and went for four byes. Time and again Jackson took the spin bowler on the pad. It was a fascinating duel between Scots.

Several critics considered that Jackson used his pads in defence rather too often. But he swung the bat to good purpose just before lunch, on-driving firmly for four and bisecting the outfielders with a juicy pull stroke. He and

Bradman seemed to be winning the initiative as the bails were lifted for lunch.

Resumption was delayed after a downpour, and while the pitch soaked up the rain the two not-out batsmen had a long and happy conversation with the Prince of Wales, whose visit to the ground had been timed badly for cricket-watching but ideally for the young Australians.

It was past three before play started, and Wyatt put Larwood and Tate on immediately. On the wet but firm pitch they created few problems for the moment. Jackson showed discretion in leaving certain balls alone, but one which he hit broke his bat, and one of the Australians caused amusement by bringing him four replacements. He made his choice and continued to pick up singles through the infield.

Peebles eventually took over from Larwood, and Hammond from Tate, and now England found the probing combination. Hammond, who always came fast off the pitch, bowled just the right length and found the spite that had eluded the other bowlers. He made one delivery kick head-high to Jackson; backs straightened. He smashed him on the glove with the next, and then on the wrist, knocking his bat from his hand. By the time the batsman had recovered, the sky was overcast, and soon after the 400 had been raised the umpires acceded to a light appeal at 3.52.

Rain fell, then the sun came out, and as the evening wore on the captains made two pitch inspections, Wyatt wanting to play, Woodfull disagreeing. It seemed there would be no further cricket when, to general amazement, a re-start was ordained for twenty-five past six – which offered one over, two at best.

Bradman and Jackson unenthusiastically made their way to the middle midst cat-calls and survived thirteen balls from Hammond and Peebles. With a measure of relief they took Australia to the shelter of 403 for 3, Bradman 130 and Jackson 43, the stand so far worth an estimable 140.

There was no rain during the night, but a heavy dew was noticeable next morning when the youngsters resumed, against Hammond and England's 'baby', Peebles. Seven singles came from the first eight overs, and a sprinkling of rain ceased before the fleeing players had even reached the pavilion.

Jackson was poised on 49 for a long time and seemed indifferent about it before hooking Leyland and running four. But Bradman cruised past his 150, and the peacefulness of the situation was disturbed only by a raucous appeal by Duckworth which seemed to startle everyone – so unrealistic was the thought that a wicket might fall.

But something strange happened at noon: the Oval pitch livened up almost supernaturally, and Hammond suddenly was able to make the ball cut and kick. Larwood came into the attack (Jackson sending Bradman scrambling deperately back into his crease from the first ball) and he, too, managed an alarming bounce off a good length. He produced an extra yard of speed in his delight at the feel of a pitch that was not docile from over-preparation.

A cynic wrote that 'neither batsman was anxious to run a sharp single in order to secure the privilege of playing him', but whenever Jackson faced up, though he took frequent shuddering blows to the body, he moved into line and never shirked.

Aubrey Faulkner, the masterly South African all-rounder, who committed suicide three weeks later, applauded the courage of both batsmen as the wicket turned hostile. Jackson, he noted, was hit on the elbow, the jaw, the hip and several times on the thighs; and he learned later that the bruises formed a black-and-blue pattern. If anything, he thought that Jackson allowed himself to be hit too often for a batsman of his class.

It was a fateful session, for Bradman's obvious discomfort against Larwood, his evasion of the flyers (especially after a sickening blow under the heart when he had made 175), and his reduced effectiveness lit a spark of hope in the minds of those Englishmen who had wondered in vain what could be done to contain him.

It is recorded that Archie Jackson told friends that George Duckworth was the first to draw attention to Bradman's hesitancy, and the scheming of the Bodyline campaign apparently began at that point.

Bradman's concern extended beyond his own person that day, for he frequently hurried to comfort his battered partner and to smack the shallow divot back into the pitch.

Together they held on, and as suddenly as it had grown murderous the pitch became placid once more, no matter how beefily the fast bowlers plunged the ball into it.

England had missed a golden opportunity.

Still there were glimpses of the best of Jackson, and still he had periodic anxieties, as when he cocked a ball between the wicketkeeper and Larwood at short leg, each leaving it to the other.

Finally, looking for his ninth boundary, but hampered by the bruised wrist, he swung imperfectly at a leg-break from Wyatt and was caught by Sutcliffe at extra cover.

The fourth-wicket partnership of 243 surpassed the record established in 1896 by Syd Gregory and Harry Trott, and Jackson's brave and disciplined 73 had helped the score to 506. His innings – and the stand – had lasted four and a half hours, and if ever an effort was worth more than face value this was it.

Bradman went on to 232 before dubiously being given out caught behind off Larwood.

Both batsmen had served their country wonderfully well.

McCabe made a daring 54, and Australia finally reached 695 – a lead of 290. There was one sad moment that evening when the 47-year-old Jack Hobbs came out to play his last innings in Test cricket and played on to Fairfax for 9. And England's sorrow was complete, after a blank fifth day, when Hornibrook bowled them out on a damaged pitch.

So Australia recaptured the Ashes on Woodfull's 33rd birthday, and youth had triumphed quite brilliantly over experience. It was Australia's first Test victory at The Oval since the 'Ashes match' back in 1882, and the cheers that greeted the appearance of Woodfull and his men on the pavilion balcony at the end rivalled those in the earlier historic contest. And lest Archie's body blows be forgotten, a newspaper cartoon depicted him, bearded in old age, recalling his innings for the benefit of a small boy: 'I got 73 runs and 540 knocks!'

He played five more matches in that summer of 1930, but was still anything but fluent. In the thriller with Gloucestershire which followed the final Test the Australians needed only 118 to win. Jackson and McCabe made half of them for the first wicket, but the remaining batsmen collapsed for a further 58 against Parker and Goddard, and the result was that great rarity – a tie.

He had other pleasant associations with Bristol to recall, for on the Sunday he made his first flight in an aeroplane, at the local Aero Club, topping it off by presenting a floral horseshoe to Winifred Brown, who had recently won the King's Cup.

The match at Canterbury was blessed by hot weather

and a wonderful demonstration of leg-spin bowling by Kent's 'Tich' Freeman. At one stage in the second innings the Australians were defending for their lives on a wearing pitch, and the parents of the boys and girls who had accompanied Bradman and Jackson excitedly to the wicket were soon barracking the batsmen. But the match was saved comfortably by a Bradman double-century and 50 not out by Jackson, whose first seven runs took an hour.

For Sussex, in a match graced not only by two Kippax hundreds, but by an appearance by another famous flyer, Amy Johnson, and copious quantities of golden wattle, Tate had Jackson caught at slip early in each innings, but not before he had given the crowd a good laugh by falling flat on his back as he made a lusty stroke to leg. His outfielding caught the eye here as well.

At Folkestone against an England XI he had to prevent a hat-trick after Kippax had fallen first ball. This he did, and the five runs he needed for his thousand for the season soon came. In an innings of 78 full of beautiful leg-glides and cover-drives, completed on his twenty-first birthday and interrupted only by a blow in the abdomen from Allom which forced him to leave the field (Allom was bowling fast enough to break McCabe's middle stump), Jackson had the perceptive wondering why he had not been one of the season's consistent major successes. The doctors were to supply one of the explanations soon enough.

And so, after the farewell dinner given by MCC, the tourists travelled north for their last match in England, at Scarborough, where a seven-inch crab was found under the pitch covers at the start of the day. Archie Jackson made 24 'pretty' runs before being bowled by a ball which pitched leg and took off, delivered by the grand and cagey old hero Wilfred Rhodes, who was playing his last first-class match; with drizzle and murky light now coming as no surprise, the Australians drew the match, and thoughts finally turned to home.

Jackson pursued the sightseeing he had promised himself all along, and in the last week of September he wrote a farewell note to a young Hampshire farmer, Harry Mills, who had befriended him:

> Five of our chaps left yesterday morning and only Hurwood and I are left at the Midland Grand. We visited the East End on Thursday last and enjoyed ourselves immensely. When you have the same experience you are going to enjoy it too. Well, Harry, as I will not see you again I do want to thank you for your many kindnesses and hope to see you again in 1934.

He had made 1097 runs, with a solitary century; was fifth in the Australian averages and aggregates; had disappointed and delighted; and had earned £600 exclusive of the 30/- a week for incidental expenses.

Mr Whitelaw's £1000 token of admiration to Don Bradman set the world champion batsman apart from all others – as if his record-breaking aggregate had not already done so. England's applause, as Geoffrey Tebbutt noted, had been ready for Jackson: 'Bradman got it, and, I fear, that which was the due of some others as well!'

CHAPTER EIGHT
FLASHES OF SUNLIGHT

Not for Archie the noisy homecoming. Having reached Melbourne, he said, 'I was breaking my neck to be home and to see my cobbers.'

So he flew on ahead of the team, and was missing when the crowds, reporters and reception party massed at Central Station on the official day of the team's arrival in Sydney. (He later apologised for any embarrassment he may inadvertently have caused.)

His mother was out shopping when he reached the house in Wrights Road, overlooking little Five Dock Bay; but the unheralded reunion soon transpired, and he had a busy time keeping up with the questions and asking his own. He spent the Saturday calling on friends, and loosened up with a few games of tennis.

The local Press finally caught up with him, and saw him as being 'in perfect health, as boyish and modest as ever'. It had been a treat, he said, to play under Woodfull's captaincy. The skipper had been popular with players and opponents alike. Grimmett was the best slow bowler in the world, without question. But Alec Hurwood, who had shared a room with Archie through most of the tour, was dreadfully unlucky.

'At no time did Hurwood bowl badly, but he just could not get wickets. Nobody could have been more popular.

79

No matter what his success or failure, he always had a smile.' (Hurwood was to play two Tests during the next summer, taking 11 wickets cheaply then disappearing from Test cricket.)

Jackson mentioned having had several tempting offers to play cricket in England, one in the Lancashire League and one with the county itself, the terms being a large lump sum, £10 a week, and employment in a solicitor's office. But he had at least one reason for refusing: 'The taxes are too heavy over there. But I am terribly keen to make the trip in 1934. I think that if I missed it I would be inclined to pack my bag and go all the same.'

A West Indies side toured Australia during that summer of 1930–31, and Archie Jackson was soon having to prove his claims for inclusion in the Test matches.

In Ryder's Testimonial at Melbourne he failed twice for the triumphant touring team against The Rest; but for NSW against the West Indians he made a pedigree 62 in the second innings, having been restored as opening batsman. It was a match set apart by the astonishing hitting of Constantine, who launched some massive sixes off Chilvers and Hunt: one landed halfway up the Hill, another onto the Hill grandstand roof and into the Showground next door, and another on to the roof of the Sheridan Stand. (Hugh Chilvers used to challenge Archie to an unusual duel on long interstate rail journeys. He would play the mouth-organ faster and faster to Archie's tapdancing, each trying to outpace and exhaust the other.)

The pitches that season turned out to be much too slow for the West Indies attack of Constantine, Griffith and Francis, and in the Test matches Learie Constantine also failed disastrously with the bat.

The tourists were crushed in the first four Tests, but, after M. A. Noble and 'Chappie' Dwyer had influenced

Adelaide, February 3, 1929: end of an epic innings: A. A. Jackson lbw White 164. The 19-year-old's years of promise had crystalised into a brave classic on his Test debut against England.

Old Charlie Bannerman, who scored 165 in the first of all Test matches, 52 years previously, congratulates the young champion who had come within one run of emulating him exactly.

Pounding the off-side field: some of Jackson's
cuts and drives during his glorious innings of
182 in the Test Trial at Sydney in December
1929.

THE AUSTRALIAN
SPORTING & DRAMATIC
NEWS

Vol. 1. No. 27.

Registered at General Post Office, Sydney, for transmission by post as a newspaper.

Subscription: 51 weeks, post free to any address in Australia, New Zealand, and Fiji, 24/-

February 9, 1929

THE YOUNG BLOOD IN OUR TEST TEAM

The two batsmen from New South Wales who represent youth in the Australian fourth Test match team: Don Bradman, on the left, and Archie Jackson, on the right.

Bradman (*left*) and Jackson were as richly promising a pair of batsmen as ever excited a cricket nation at the same time. How could anyone have foreseen the contrasting destinies?

A proud and modest cricketer: Archie's memento to a friend in England.

'Nice piece of cloth, Bertie.' Jackson admires wicketkeeper Oldfield's blazer after kitting out for the 1930 tour of England.

Jackson drives for his long-awaited century on English soil, in the Australians' match against Somerset at Taunton. 'The sun had thawed him out.'

Bill Woodfull (*left*), Australia's captain, takes Archie Jackson to open with him against Lancashire at Old Trafford. The 20-year-old made 52 in two hours.

Another entry, this time with an omen as Jackson's bat slips from his grasp.
This match at Bristol in August 1930 finished thrillingly in a tie after openers
Jackson and McCabe had made half of the Australians' requirement of only 118.

The Oval, 1930. Jackson, sweating it out against England on a sometimes spiteful pitch, is struck yet again, an agonising blow on the hipbone from a ball flung down by Larwood, the Notts express. Jackson (73) helped Bradman add 243 for the fourth Australian wicket.

Photographic record of a brief innings: this ball (seen as a blur) was possibly the one that cost Jackson his wicket for one run in the 1930 Headingley Test match. He was caught by Larwood at short leg. Duckworth is the wicketkeeper, and Chapman, England's captain, is at point. Jackson's dismissal let in Bradman, who scored 309 not out that day.

Bradman (232) gets a pull shot away during the famous stand at The Oval, Jackson his partner backing up. To England's 405, Australia replied with 695 and went on to an innings victory that brought back the Ashes.

With all the balance of a ballet dancer Jackson swings a ball from Peebles away during the Oval Test, his last on English soil.

The great adventure over, Archie Jackson calls to see his mother, the first-hand accounts of the English tour being much preferred to the slow-travelling handwritten letters.

Australia v West Indies, Sydney, February 1931. Jackson was 12th man. Back row: R. K. Oxenham, J. E. D. Sealy, W. H. Ponsford, G. A. Headley, A. A. Jackson, H. C. Griffith, K. E. Rigg, G. N. Francis; middle row: S. J. McCabe, I. Barrow, A. G. Fairfax, O. G. Scott, H. Ironmonger, C. A. Roach, W. A. S. Oldfield, E. L. Bartlett; front: H. Armstrong (umpire), D. G. Bradman, F. R. Martin, A. F. Kippax, G. C. Grant (West Indies captain), W. M. Woodfull (Australian captain), L. S. Birkett, C. V. Grimmett, L. N. Constantine, W. G. French (umpire).

April 1932, and Archie Jackson (centre), forced by his illness to give up the strenuous demands of big cricket, is reunited with team-mates Don Bradman (right) and Jack Fingleton.

Putting on a brave face, Jackson poses for the camera at Calvary Hospital, Adelaide, in 1932, as his battle against insidious disease continues.

Lovers stalked by impending tragedy: Archie and his petite fiancée Phyllis Thomas.

Letter to a friend: a typically optimistic message from his mountain retreat, in handwriting as stylish as his batsmanship.

A *Sydney Mail* photograph, February 22, 1933: 'A large crowd witnessed the departure of the funeral from the former international's old home, and thousands attended the Field of Mars, where Archie Jackson was laid to rest.'

Bill Hunt tends his old pal's grave, 40 years on.

the preparation of the pitch at Sydney for the fifth contest, they won their first Test against Australia, with Martin and the great George Headley, both Jamaicans, scoring hundreds, and the fast battery taking advantage of a rain-soaked pitch – a near-miraculous reversal.

By then Archie Jackson had lost his place after three failures at Sydney, Brisbane and Melbourne. In this fifth Test he came in as runner for an injured batsman on the final afternoon. It was the last time he set foot on the field in first-class cricket.

Outside the Tests he had been quite successful, and he was certainly no failure in the first Test, at Adelaide, a ground of happy memories for him. Here, in the first-ever Australia–West Indies match, he (70 not out) and Ponsford hit off the 170 needed for victory without being separated – this after Kippax had proudly made the maiden century of the series in the first innings. Umpire Hele recalled: 'As they walked out together, Jackson said to Ponsford, "I see the skipper is padded up. We won't give him a hit!"'

Ponsford, Woodfull and Bradman dominated the rest of the rubber, and Jackson, being favoured to Woodfull as opener until the fourth Test, had to stomach three successive failures before the selectors' axe inevitably fell.

He had been forced to leave the field through illness on the third day of the Brisbane Test, and missed the State match with Victoria immediately following.

His reappearance for the fourth Test, at Melbourne – a two-day affair in which he took four catches and Constantine dismissed him for 15 – was his final big match. He was too sick to play for NSW against the tourists a week later, and was understandably relegated to 12th man for the final Test.

The only other performances he had to look back on

with pleasure that season were a splendid 166 as part of a record 334 stand with Bradman in the Shield match at Adelaide (when Bill Hunt bowled very effectively), and an earlier 53 at Brisbane in a match of gargantuan scoring, Cecil Thompson topping it off with 275 not out.

And it was here in Brisbane that Archie met and fell for Phyllis Thomas.

Frank Gough, the Queensland all-rounder, introduced them at a tennis party over the weekend. Phyllis was only eighteen, and, having been trained in ballet, had found success in Sydney with an adagio dance act with her brother Ray. Hardly 5 ft tall, she had the gaiety and sparkle that matched Archie's temperament perfectly.

Though most at home on stage, she loved cricket, probably owing her enthusiasm to her mother. Mrs Thomas, who as a girl in Bendigo had lived next door to Harry Trott, the old Australian captain, had always been keen on the game, and for a number of years helped prepare the players' teas at Windsor Park, where Northern Suburbs played.

So Brisbane now lured Archie Jackson with a romantic appeal beyond anticipation.

He was working at Anthony Horderns now, and drawing large crowds to the Sydney store to watch him bat in the nets. He had made a little extra money by putting his name on Surridge bats, though it seems his addiction to an old favourite that refused to wear out prevented him from actually using one.

Bill Hunt kept that bat of Archie's, and used to draw attention to a flaw along the inside edge – a split which, if hit, would surely cause several inches to flake away: 'But he didn't edge 'em down the leg side. He might've got out in the slips occasionally, but his leg glances were perfect. Really perfect!'

The blade has a concave at the meat which tells of a thousand accurate strokes, and the perished rubber grip resembles an aerial view of the Amazon delta, just to remind its handler that much time has passed since it was unwrapped and given its preparatory oiling. It is a rousing relic.

The stricken cricketer picked up in health sufficiently to take part in a 'missionary' tour of North Queensland in March 1931 with a collection of players led by Alan Kippax, and showing extraordinary stamina and application, he broke Victor Trumper's 'record' of 1046 runs by 163. He came back sunburnt and apparently fit and well, even though it had been an arduous expedition.

They travelled for almost a week to reach their starting point – Cairns – sailing via Brisbane and Townsville, and motoring through the thick tropical country of the Atherton Tablelands, along one twelve-mile stretch of road which, someone dazedly discovered, incorporated 602 bends. On Malanda's concrete wicket Jackson made 61.

This he followed with 158 (the last 50 in ten minutes) and 51 not out (in eight minutes) at Cairns, delighting the capacity crowd and playing through showers of rain that could only have exacerbated his condition.

Runs were three-a-minute all through the tour, and the light-hearted cricket of Kippax, Bradman, McCabe, Jackson, Fairfax and Wendell Bill filled the collection boxes and provided a nett profit of £3000 which in due course was laid out on turf pitches and general improvements. The stars were paid ten shillings a day against loss of salary, and all travelling and accommodation expenses.

From Cairns they moved on to Innisfail, the centre of the sugar industry, where the townsfolk were complaining of a dry summer. The night after the team left ten inches of rain fell – a phenomenon which might well have added to their mystique.

More of Archie's letters survive from this period. One, written from Innisfail, is disarmingly frank:

> Our tour up here has been most pleasant, though I dislike intensely our present abode. It's such a wet town, and it makes you feel miserable. The rainfall per year is 140", about 110" more than we receive in Sydney over the same period. It rains nine months a year, and the population comprises the most cosmopolitan crowd in Australia, so it's rotten!
>
> Our first game against Eacham at Malanda was very funny. The grass was long and wet so that to score a boundary the ball had to be lifted. Anyway, they batted first and reached 141. Kippax sent the other chaps in to keep their wickets intact so as we could bat in the afternoon. However, before long four were down for 15.
>
> Then Fairfax went in (you know – the strong man!) to stop the rot. The first ball hit him on the gloves and he got one run. When he got up the other end the bowler hit him on the pad and he was given out. He certainly did perform, and spent the rest of the day plastering butter on the bruise. Kippax 32, Bradman 34 and myself 61, managed to evade defeat. The next match against Cairns was high-scoring. Bradman scored 103 and 90 and I got 158 and 50 n.o.
>
> Last night a dance was held in our honour and the entire town turned out. We were kicked all over the body. It was so rough that Alan Fairfax reckoned he scored the final try just on time!

A sidelight of the match at Malanda was Jackson's planting of a tree to mark the team's visit. A leaf from the tree was later sent to Phyl, who placed it in a small scrapbook, where it remains a sweet link with a merry cricket tour long ago.

A seven-hour train journey had the players in Townsville for two two-day matches, the second, against a North Queensland representative XI, seeing four centuries from the NSW side – Jackson 172. Then, after traversing more jungle, canefields and banana plantations, they played on Ayr's new turf pitch, where Bradman made the match his own, scoring 107 and taking 6 for 23.

Another frenzied welcome at Bowen turned to delight in another massacre by the touring players. This time McCabe, Kippax and Jackson made centuries.

They travelled overnight to Mackay and ran into more heavy rain, then left at 4.30 in the morning for another long, tiring haul to Rockhampton and, at last, three days' freedom, most of which was spent at the beach. They were still nineteen days from Brisbane, the last stop. Bradman had the misfortune – or merciful fortune – to sprain his ankle (not for the last time) in a hole at mid-on during the Rockhampton match, and had to remain behind.

But the fireworks continued at Gympie, where McCabe belted 173, including 40 off an over. By the time they reached Ipswich most of them were exhausted, and Archie Jackson poured it all out in another letter to Bill:

Our tour of Nth Queensland has now concluded, and thank goodness! It has been rather a bore from start to finish, particularly as we had to attend so many dinners, socials, dances, etc, and in every case finance was the ideal. I would never make this trip again unless I was guaranteed £100, and that's not enough!

With all due modesty, I have had a most successful tour and have scored 1100 runs average 93.00, with six centuries. I am, of course, heading both aggregate and average, and may just possibly scrape together another century before the tour definitely concludes.

I was extremely disappointed at the failure of Balmain in the last two rounds, but I'm sure they will do much better next year.

You certainly had a particularly pleasant season, and you surely must be given a chance against the Sth Africans. If, because of the exchange, they cannot fulfil their itinerary in Australia, it is quite possible that we may go to Africa. How would you like the trip, Bill? It would certainly be a great one from every point of view, and if you were one of the tourists it would make you a star.

What have you to tell me that is so interesting regarding the girl opposite? Have you arranged our wedding, or merely fixed our engagement? However I am still interested. After all it is most likely worth exploring.

Well, Bill, I must close now, but would like to tell you that Alan Fairfax stated he is dying to meet Balmain next season just for the satisfaction of cracking you over the fence a few times. Still, I don't think he could crack me!

It was a happy, hopeful, teasing letter from a man full of the joys of living.

CHAPTER NINE

SUMMER ENDS

He kept in trim during the 1931 winter with plenty of golf and tennis, which also helped keep his mind off the economic crisis. The Government Savings Bank had frozen depositors' funds, and so tight was the situation that he had to decline the offer of his friend Harry Mills to send a gift of a wireless from England because of the excise duty of £15 payable in Sydney.

Harry sent the set all the same, and in the letter of thanks Archie remarked on the mildness of the Australian winter: 'It is to be hoped that summer proves just as mild. Sometimes we get some hellish heatwaves that make a fellow pine for the cold of England, though people are never satisfied, are they?'

His recurring sickness, still only at the nuisance level and not yet diagnosed as anything critical, had lapsed once more into inertia as the 1931–32 cricket season opened, though at least one friend was struck by the profusion of medicine bottles in Archie's room.

He made a lot of runs on a country tour with Alan Kippax's side, and when he played a showpiece innings of 183 for Balmain – his highest ever – against Gordon he and his supporters had every hope and expectation that he would feature prominently for State and country against the visiting South Africans.

He was selected for the opening Sheffield Shield match of the season and travelled with the team to Brisbane, but having just recovered from a bout of influenza he had the misfortune to be caught in a rain-squall while crossing the Hawkesbury River, and his chest ailment was activated.

Phyl sat with her lunch-box and clapped with the crowd as the NSW players took the field at Brisbane; then she noticed Archie was not among them, and as she was wondering what could have happened to him Alan Fairfax came over and broke the news that Archie had brought up blood, collapsed and been rushed to hospital. Would she get some pyjamas for him?

It was a dreadful shock, and both teams were plunged into heavy gloom when the NSW manager told them.

The emergency dealt with, a sensational match ensued: Eddie Gilbert, the Aboriginal, bowling with lethal speed and bounce, dismissed Bradman for a duck, and Kippax suffered a jagged cut on the temple after mis-hooking Thurlow (and finished up in the next hospital bed to Archie's, according to *Australian Cricketer* magazine). McCabe played what he always considered the innings of his life, rising from his team's desperate plight to score an undefeated 229; and Jackson's replacement, Jack Fingleton, made a dour 93.

Jackson, who, to judge from a later letter, believed himself to be a flu victim, was discharged from hospital after five days and returned to Sydney with the team.

Within a week, at the instigation of the Board of Control, Archie was installed in Bodington Sanitorium at Wentworth Falls in the Blue Mountains. It was announced that he would not be playing cricket in the foreseeable future.

Bill Hunt and his fiancée, Ann, made the journey to see him at every opportunity, and took him on the bus into

Springwood for tea – as much as anything to release him from the coughing and spitting all around him.

He was frustrated beyond description. He wanted letters from friends, yet those same letters drew his spirit down to the lowlands that he loved. He needed the companionship of his mates and parents and of Phyl.

After a few months in the institution he felt compelled to find an abode of his own. So he took a cottage, 'Tranmere', in The Mall at Leura, and there sister Peggie joined him for the remainder of the summer and through the winter of 1932.

In April he broke away briefly to Sydney and called in on 'Johnnie' Moyes, then sports editor of the *Sun*. Moyes wrote hopefully: 'I have not seen him since his return from Brisbane, stricken with the illness that caused his withdrawal from cricket. The change was remarkable. Then he looked the sick man that he was. Now he has about him an air of health, activity, and optimism. Will he play again next season? Time alone will tell, but the delightful batsman is full of hope.'

It happened that Bradman and Fingleton also walked in moments later, and Moyes speculated on the possibility of the three of them heading the NSW batting line-up before long.

Several other times Jackson slipped away from his mountain retreat and appeared without warning on the doorstep at home or at Bill Hunt's place. His parents were gently understanding, but Mr Hunt senior, who cherished him as would a father, withheld his pleasure at seeing him and adopted what he felt was the only fit attitude: 'Go back to Leura, Archie. We don't want to see you down here till you're well again. Come back when you're cured and you'll be as welcome as the day is long.'

In January Bill Hunt received his Test invitation, at the

bottom of which was a postscript from W. C. Bull to the effect that Dr Collins had recently examined Archie and found him to be making 'excellent progress'.

In a letter to Harry Mills in May Archie stated his aims clearly enough:

> I should dearly love to play against the Englishmen next season, so can only hope for the best. I've quite decided on another visit to England in 1934, whether as a member of the Aust. XI or not so ... less than two years hence too! Perhaps I'll qualify for a county – who knows! I would like to spend a few years in England. What a time we'd have. By that time I would be nearly 25 years of age ... at all events old enough to paint dear old London red.

Clarifying his state of health, he explained to his friend:

> I had a severe breakdown, contracted pleurisy, and for a few weeks my life was in jeopardy. However I managed to pull through and am depending on my present sedentary existence to completely restore me to my usual state of health.

At the time of writing it was 'frightfully cold', and he was spending the greater part of each day curled up in front of the fire reading.

He went on to express concern for Alan Fairfax, who was finding little success with Accrington in the Lancashire League, and lamented his own wicked luck in having to miss the tour of Arthur Mailey's side through Canada and America: 'Still, it is probably for the best, and after all I'll see America even if I have to wait for a few years.'

Turning to the dismissal of the Lang State Government, he was inclined towards a feeling of relief: 'Lang has created a good deal of turmoil and strife, and almost any change must be for the best. Stevens, the new leader, is a fine type of man and has already gained the confidence of the people.'

Among more mundane matters he asked Harry to send him a couple of cheap grey hats, size $6\frac{7}{8}$: 'Australian hats have a larger brim than the English, and as I have the brim down I look like a cowboy.'

In part-exchange he was going to send a bat: 'It was used twice against the Englishmen in Tests and three times against the West Indies as well as a few State games, so it's quite a warrior.'

A later letter, in August, revealed that he planned to sail for England in April 1933, 'but I can't say anything further at the moment.'

He was still concerned about the weather, which had been unusually cold, but was looking forward to some fun in the snow which lay thick over the mountains.

Correspondence between the NSWCA, Archie and various doctors, which came to light as recently as 1983, reveals the tug of war between the authorities on one hand who believed the sanitorium was the only place for the sick batsman, and the young cricketer himself, who was desperate to get away. 'I find it almost impossible to consume my food with fellow patients,' he wrote plaintively. He had 'implicit confidence' in Dr McIntosh at Leura. He was 'facing my position more squarely by entering his supervision and have absolute faith in the knowledge that my cure will be complete.'

He considered the attitude of Dr Collins, the Board's medical advisor, 'unfair and unjust': 'he is not infallible and I shall certainly prove him wrong'. Dr Collins wanted him to stay at Bodington for a further three months.

'Do be patient, Archie,' wrote A. W. Green, a NSWCA committee member, who pointed out that to have the disease under control was one thing; but it could be subject to 're-infection'.

In another letter, to Bill Hunt, Archie claimed that Dr McIntosh had told him he was out of danger, and should be able to play against England in the 1932–33 series. His greatest fear was of 'contracting the germ once again' while in the sanitorium.

The risk that he would forfeit the financial support of the NSWCA was ever present, though a letter reveals that, having left Bodington, he was granted £3.3.0 a week, for which he expressed profuse gratitude. He also told Green that he now weighed 10 st 8 lbs, 3 lb up on his weight upon arrival.

In July 1932, NSWCA secretary Heydon wrote to Archie in Calvary Hospital, Adelaide, asking about his financial situation. The Association were debating whether to continue with the grant. Heydon also wrote to Dr McIntosh, who explained that Archie had gone to Adelaide, with his 'permission', for treatment to his skin condition, which had worsened. Dr McIntosh assured the committee that he felt Archie was 'playing the game'.

Heydon's next piece of news came via a telegram from Archie in Adelaide. 'Your letter delayed,' it read. 'Had five hundred and fifty six months ago, now three hundred and ninety. Letter following.'

He wrote that his health was 'really splendid', and he expected to participate in at least a few first-class games next season. Umpire George Hele had been to see him, as had some of the South Australian players, the main topic of conversation being whether Australia would retain the Ashes against Jardine's England team. He had an occasional net, and renewed other friendships, one being with Minnie Rosman, an elderly spinster who had been his 'South Australian mother'.

Then came a letter which must have struck the NSWCA committee like a thunderbolt. It was a confidential report from a physician in Adelaide, who stated that Archie Jackson, while in Calvary Hospital, 'expectorated a small quantity of blood. The examination of his sputum showed very numerous tubercle bacilli'. Clinical examination showed that he had 'pneumonary tuberculosis with fairly extensive involvement of the lungs'.

The doctor at Leura seemed satisfied with his recovery, and Archie began to think in terms of returning to civilisation. But it still needed time – plenty of time. He was impatient. He wanted to be with Phyl again. So he formulated the plan to live in Brisbane, where the hotter climate, in his misguided opinion, would promote his restoration.

As a new summer dawned he released himself from his mountain exile and took up the threads of living once more.

Moving up the latitudes to Brisbane, he spent some time at Brookstead, 140 miles away and drought-stricken. In a letter to Heydon he explained that his health was 'perfectly good' and that the northern clime seemed to be beneficial as his weight was now 10 st 10$\frac{1}{2}$lbs. A few days later the NSWCA wrote to him to say that his allowance would cease in a fortnight. He wrote expressing his thanks and saying that he had been offered a position in Queensland.

Meanwhile, the Adelaide physician had been asked to report on Archie's condition yet again. His view was brighter this time, though he warned that he could not play serious cricket without 'very harmful results following'. He had agreed to Archie's move to Queensland so long as he took great care of himself – and returned to the Blue Mountains for the summer.

Finally came Archie's reassurance, in a letter of thanks to A. W. Green of the NSWCA, that he expected to regain his health completely while up north, but would return one day to his home State 'and again don the blue cap'.

Countless hopes and prayers were with him as he whitened his cricket boots again. Eric Barbour summed it up in the *Sydney Mail*, recalling Jackson's 'body blows from Tate and Larwood that might well have daunted a Carnera'. He wrote: 'We all hope that the gallant pluck that carried Archie through this searching test will help him to throw off his present illness, and that we shall soon see him resume the place in the Australian XI that he has so honestly won.'

The incredible fact is that, having offered his services to Northern Suburbs, he proceeded – though fearfully short of breath – to make a staggering number of runs. It is worth recounting his full performances on a country tour and in Brisbane in 1932–33: 104, 60, 100, 53 not out, 56 not out, 66 not out, 37, 17, 155 (in a Queensland trial match), 105 not out, 14, 124 not out, and 77.

His seven innings for Northern Suburbs drew record crowds, and left him with an average of 159.66 after batting against such opponents as Oxenham, Hornibrook, Gilbert, Thurlow and Gamble.

It was eye-opening, but there are old club cricketers in Brisbane still who remember how it was cutting away his life. One, Tom O'Shea, of the Valley club, off whom Jackson scored his last century, recalled it as 'a delightful, pathetic innings. Delightful in his strokemaking against our weak attack but pathetic to witness his suffering. I vividly recall his state of exhaustion when he had to hurry between wickets. He'd spar for time by bending down to adjust his pads. Goodness knows how many his innings was worth had he been able to run for all available runs.'

Alan McGilvray recalled how in one of Archie's last innings in Sydney grade cricket the fielding side faced the agonising dilemma of whether to run-out the gasping out-of-breath Jackson to save him further exhaustion, or to spare him so that his obsessive but self-destructive love of batting could continue to be gratified: a harrowing choice of mercies.

He was staying at the home of Phyl's parents in Old Sandgate Road, Clayfield, his emigration north apparently having been made rather hastily. On October 2, he wrote to Bill to apologise:

Terribly sorry I was unable to get over to the 'Main and say Au Revoir to you prior to my departure to Brisbane, but was so busy was unable to do so. Know you will forgive me.

Started grade cricket yesterday, Count, and on a wet wicket too. Nth Suburbs played Toombul. We had first knock and scored 101 of which I contributed 56 not out. Toombul have lost nine for 87, so the position is extremely interesting....

A crowd of over 2000 watched the game – a record for Brisbane pennant cricket. Like Noodles Fairfax, my personality is magnetic – oh yeh?

Bought a car the other day, Bill – a Chrysler Roadster, and quite a good job too. Paid £165 cash for it, but believe me it's worth it. So, m'lud, when you come north with the State team I'll only charge you a bob a mile. How does that suit you, eh?

Start in the Brisbane Sports Depot tomorrow. Coach in the afternoon, and I think I'll be contributing weekly articles to the *Daily Mail*. The Brisbane public will shortly be wondering who this Bill Hunt is.

By the way, Count, you might send up the Walter Hammond bat if you have no further use for it. Should imagine it is still good for a few more hundreds.

He proceeded, in fact, to work as advisory sales assistant at Johnson's Sports Depot in Queen Street (also sponsoring their brand of cricket boot), to act as assistant coach to the QCA, and to write regularly for the *Mail*.

He and Phyl spent a lot of time together, and from the wings of the theatre he often watched her act. When she attracted prolonged applause one evening he chuckled: 'For a moment I thought it was me out there!'

He spent more time reading, and started Lowell Thomas's *With Lawrence in Arabia* in December.

There was a longing throughout the nation for him to return to big cricket, and only the selectors' sense of responsibility kept him out. The Press clamoured for his inclusion in the exploratory Australian XIs that played Jardine's MCC team at Perth and Melbourne, for though it had been decided that he was as yet ineligible for Queensland, a longish innings against Larwood, Voce, Bowes, Allen and company could have warranted his return to the Test side.

But it was reported in mid-November that he was thought unlikely to be able to take the strain of a four-day match, and therefore had not been considered.

E. A. Shaw, Queensland's manager, was certain that he hadn't the strength to endure a gruelling first-class match. Archie, of course, felt otherwise.

He wrote to a friend in England that he felt strong and was certain he would be fit enough to play, 'but one never knows what is lurking around the corner'.

To Harry Mills he wrote on the last day of October 1932 that he had already made nearly 700 runs, but 'unfortunately, though, I have violated a Board of Control rule re writing for the Press, so I don't suppose I'll be allowed to participate in the Tests this season. Still, old chap, the game must take second place to a man's living.'

His plans had, of necessity, been modified already: 'Oh, by the way, Harry, I'm a Queenslander these days. I came up here for health reasons and will probably stay for a season or two.'

He was concerned at Queensland's poor showing against Victoria, but felt there was something he could do about it: 'I am available against Victoria later in the year, so hope to strengthen the batting. You see, one has to reside in a State for three months before playing, and I've only been here about two months. Naturally, Harry, now that I'm residing in Queensland I will not be able to go to England in March next. However, I fully expect to get back into the Australian XI and visit England again in 1934. So, old chap, look out for me then.'

His writings in the *Mail* reflected an acute insight and, expectedly, a sensibility. He noted in the cricket of his adopted State 'a most pronounced inferiority complex (that) will, unless eradicated, tend to retard the progress of Queensland cricket.'

In a coaching article he wrote pungently and characteristically that 'the late-cut, perfectly executed, is the most delightful yet most dangerous stroke in the game.'

Recalling his many country tours through both States 'in an endeavour to unearth another Trumper or Turner', he turned his attention to the country lads who came to Brisbane for trials. Don Tallon, of Bundaberg, he thought, 'may emulate the deeds with bat and gloves of Les Ames of Kent', and of Eddie Gilbert, the Aborigine: 'having batted against him on three occasions, I have no hesitation in declaring his delivery fair and above suspicion'.

As the Ashes battle loomed he urged the inclusion of younger players, preferring Fleetwood-Smith ('the very man to rout the Englishmen') to Ironmonger, O'Reilly to Oxenham, and probably having more faith in Lonergan

97

than the recently battered Kippax. He felt Ponsford would be of more use to Australia batting down the order.

He was so much inclined towards youth that he gave every impression that he considered Grimmett to be just about finished: 'It has been gradually forced upon our senses that Grimmett is a back number, and is being carried in the team.'

'Scarlet', of course, lasted several years more, surviving a barren series now, but taking large bundles of wickets in England and South Africa. But Jackson was quite excited by a Queensland spinner named Jack Govan, who had some moments of glory, particularly when he bowled Woodfull.

'If Govan is ever selected to tour England with an Australian XI, he will realise that the reward for his perseverance is indeed great. Money cannot buy a trip home with an Australian XI, and the happy memories last for ever.'

Soon he found himself in the strange position of watching from the Press-box as Alan Kippax made 179 for NSW against Queensland, and, bold pupil, tendering advice. 'He should continue to bat brilliantly, and not concentrate too much on defence' – perhaps less trite than it appears.

In the same match Archie's old schoolmate, Syd Hird, also made a century, the merit of which was loyally drawn to the attention of the Australian selectors, though he later felt compelled to reproach Hird for his 'unimpressive' bowling.

Sometimes his claims were a shade extravagant. In listing four promising Brisbane cricketers he wrote: 'These young players look better than Don Bradman did when he first strolled on the Sydney Cricket Ground, a novice of the willow, but today a potentate of the game.'

Yet all he desired was to encourage, encourage, encourage.

He raised his hands in horror at the thought of veterans O'Connor and Thompson returning to the Queensland side, and asserted that withdrawal from the Sheffield Shield competition would be a preferable course until suitable young blood could be found.

By the middle of January the Test series had reached fever pitch. England's Bodyline bowling attack had divided the country into one multitudinous, offended protest group on the one hand, and on the other a minority who felt the tactics would not necessarily kill off the game of cricket and several participants with it.

Archie Jackson, unhappily, belonged to the minority. Unhappily because in his indisposition he seemed like the retired old warrior telling the tyros how it should be done. It was general knowledge that he had never been short on courage himself, but although it can never be known just how he would have dealt with the hostile leg-side attack, the fact remains that he was unable to demonstrate his point of view in a practical way.

He was utterly sincere in his belief that Larwood and Voce could be played and scored from, and on his death-bed he told his friends repeatedly that the Australians simply needed to accelerate their footwork. For a time he nurtured hopes that he would have an opportunity to prove his notion.

Nevertheless, his views were sought and he simply had to go to press with an opinion one way or another. True to himself as ever, he wrote what he believed. His criticism of certain players may have stung, but three weeks later it fell into perspective as it became apparent that the opinions were those of a young man whose lifeblood was draining rapidly away.

'Other writers have said that Ponsford and Fingleton have been battered unmercifully about the body. That is mostly their own fault ... Fingleton, like Woodfull, is a flat-footed batsman ... Bradman and McCabe, on the other hand, have hardly felt the impact of leather on flesh, primarily because their movements are snappy enough to allow them to glide to the off side and allow the balls to fly harmlessly by ... I have always believed, and still do, that Richardson is not a Test match player ... For the sake of Australia's sporting traditions, may it be left to the cricketers themselves to furnish the only answer to the legitimate tactics employed by the Englishmen ... It is my belief that Larwood would not intentionally hurt a fly.'

Very few people in Australia in January 1933 would have been prepared to accept the tailpiece.

On February 10, 1933 the fourth Test match began at Brisbane, but Archie Jackson was not there to see it. Early in the month he collapsed after playing cricket, and was taken to Ingarfield Private Hospital. He had batted with a runner in most of his later innings, 'Cassie' Andrews, another NSW exile, being the last to escort him.

With tuberculosis rife in both lungs, he was sinking before Phyl's helpless gaze. And so, sensing they would never have the chance of marrying, but reflecting that doctors at times had been mistaken, they announced their betrothal a week after her twenty-first birthday.

Phyl, her heart breaking, kept up her nightly and matinee ballet performances in the Minstrel Show at the Regent Theatre and came faithfully to the hospital straight after the curtain, usually with her stage make-up sustaining facial cheer.

Back in Balmain unawareness suddenly had turned to alarm as a 'come quick' telegram arrived. Mrs Jackson set out on the long train journey north, and Archie's father and family friends, the Walkers, followed. Bill Hunt flew to Brisbane with the famous aviator P. G. Taylor a week later. Archie, having suffered a severe haemorrhage, was in a very poor state when he arrived.

As that decisive Test match was played out in a heat-wave Bill read the newspaper reports to his dying friend while Australia tottered towards another defeat.

'I want to get back, Bill,' he gasped.

A number of players visited him, including Woodfull, Ponsford, Darling, Bromley, Duckworth, Arthur Mailey, and MCC manager 'Plum' Warner. And of all Harold Larwood's many mementoes one item – a slip of paper – remains more precious than any other: a telegram of congratulation from Archie Jackson dated February 15.

He was hardly ever alone in those last days. A local Methodist minister, H. M. Wheller, saw him daily, and on his second-last visit he read him the 23rd Psalm, his favourite. They talked briefly and then prayed, and as the minister departed Archie raised his eyes and said, 'Thank you. That has meant a great deal to me.'

Later when his mother came back into the room he whispered that he was happy.

The relatives looked on helplessly as the flaxen-haired young man lay still, fighting weakly for breath. On the Wednesday afternoon he rallied slightly and wanted to know the Test score.

Australia, he was told, had fallen right away in their second innings.

He sank into a deep sleep.

Fifteen minutes after midnight on February 16, 1933, Archie Jackson's fight for life came to an end. The mourning was to last many years.

CHAPTER TEN

A MAN CAN ONLY FIGHT

The unsuspecting Australian people, who had watched him develop and placed so much hope on his delicate form, were stunned by the news of his death. Those close to him had feared the worst for some time, and to them the reality was harrowing, hardly diminishing as the months passed.

Johnnie Moyes, who remembered him as a fifteen-year-old at Chatswood Oval batting against Macartney and Kelleway with eye-catching aplomb, wrote that 'all the disasters which have befallen our cricketers in the field are now as nothing compared with the loss to cricket of this great exponent of the game.'

He spoke for the nation. But the grief was at two levels, and to those who had known Archie Jackson well there seemed neither justification nor meaning in his fate. It led some to question their beliefs.

But it was one moment inevitable, the next a thing of the past. In proof the flags at the 'Gabba were at half-mast and the players and umpires wore black arm-bands on the final day of the Test match, though some must still have felt that the pale, smiling face was looking out at them from the pavilion shadows.

Alan Kippax, who was making daily broadcasts on the Tests, had the opportunity of paying his tribute to both

Australian and English radio audiences.

For a day the casket remained at the Thomas home, then on the Friday at South Brisbane station Phyl's brother and father and Bill Hunt assisted as pall-bearers, carrying their burden to the train past a silent assembly.

In a kind of Viking glory Archie Jackson's remains were taken back to Sydney in the same coach of the mail train that conveyed his parents and the solemn Test cricketers of both countries.

A large gathering awaited the train at Central early on the Saturday, and as the cortege passed Gladesville Reserve, where a match was in progress, the cricketers broke off play to circle the pitch in bareheaded homage.

At the Jackson home in Wrights Road an enormous assemblage of people waited quietly outside the house and along the street, boys with bats and stumps limp in their hands, adults, some curious, some weeping openly or within.

A brief service was conducted in the home, and then in mid-morning the mile-long cortege moved off for the Field of Mars Cemetery, through dense crowds that had begun to form hours earlier along Victoria Road and Lyons Road, three- or four-deep most of the way.

The scene at the cemetery was also Valentino-like in its fervid confusion as the coffin, preceded by members of the Haberfield Lodge, to which Archie had belonged, was slowly borne to the graveside.

The Rev. Sam McKibbin had travelled especially from Singleton – it had been one of Archie's dying wishes – and he now delivered a touching address.

The pall-bearers who carried Archie to his final rest were all Test cricketers, his kinsmen until so recently: Bill Woodfull, Vic Richardson, Don Bradman, Bert Oldfield, Stan McCabe, and Bill Ponsford. Alan Kippax replaced

McCabe at the graveside when he became ill.

The cemetery, next to the orchards where Archie 'scrumped' apples as a boy, had never known such a sea of mourners. They came from miles around despite the long walk.

There were numerous cricketers, and representatives of all branches of sport and business, in Balmain, throughout the State, and all Australia. Rozelle Public School had paraded *en masse* and observed a silence, and the boys' wreath was accompanied by a letter of condolence which, with all the other cards and letters (and a cable from Alan Fairfax, who now lived in England), filled an album three inches thick. That, of course, was only a symbol of the uttered sympathy, and took no account of the sorrow felt by a million anonymous citizens.

Even the newsboys who sold papers at the Sydney Cricket Ground took up a collection and within minutes had thirty shillings for a wreath.

Anthony Horderns, no longer able to offer the populace batting displays by their hero, set aside a special window as a memorial, with his portrait, stumps, a bat and wreath draped in velvet.

It was a time to reflect on past events and conversations. Eddie Shaw, who wrote for the *Telegraph* as 'Third Man', could not forget Archie's fighting spirit. Only days before being rushed to hospital for the last time he had told Shaw that he felt the cards were stacked against him. 'But, with a characteristic smile, he added: "A man can only fight this thing out; if he wins it has been worthwhile; if he goes under, well, he at heart feels that what is to be will be." '

Bill Woodfull, in making public his sorrow, remarked on Jackson's 'happy optimism' when he and some other players visited him in hospital.

Don Bradman, in a radio tribute, remembered how,

four years earlier almost to the day, they had batted together against England at Adelaide in a vain effort to stave off defeat. He believed him to have been a batting genius.

At a memorial service held at Balmain Central Methodist Mission, 'Plum' Warner ascended the pulpit and delivered a touching address which was relayed by loudspeaker to the crowds outside and broadcast through 2BL. Woodfull, Kippax and Mailey also spoke.

The congregation sang *Jesu, Lover of My Soul*, a hymn so often sung by Archie to his own piano accompaniment; he had told his mother frequently 'there is no hymn quite like this'.

A letter written by Archie on January 23 and sent seamail reached Harry Mills in England almost a month after the world had learned of his death.

'England, to my way of thinking,' Archie had written, 'will win the Ashes in Brisbane.'

He referred to Larwood as 'a devastating whirlwind', and noted that 'the Australian batsmen are beginning to squeal – certainly a rotten thing to say – but it's a fact and is creating a good deal of unnecessary trouble.'

He explained his absence from the Queensland side: 'It is too late in the season. I want to start off fresh next season ... I had another knock yesterday, the first for five weeks. I scored 77 in 94 minutes, so am still in pretty good form.' That was to be his final innings.

On September 3, as the result of a public subscription, a red granite headstone, designed by former Test cricketer Tommy Andrews, who was a monumental mason, was unveiled by the NSW premier B.S.B. Stevens. He addressed a very large company of people, Phyl among them, and said that they had come to pay homage to a great spirit, to one who had left behind him 'the best things a man can leave: the reputation of friendship, of sonship, of devotion to his home and to his church.'

The sum of £453 had been subscribed, some of it through a vaudeville concert at the Cremorne Theatre in Brisbane in which Australian middle-weight boxer Ron Richards gave a sparring exhibition and Phyl and her brother danced, and some from a fast-scoring match between two star-studded sides at Sydney Cricket Ground, whose ground staff worked voluntarily.

After the purchase of the memorial stone the residue, £357, was handed to Archie's parents.

The Balmain club set up an Archie Jackson Memorial Shield to be awarded to the most successful of its grade teams each season; the initial winners were the 2nd XI in 1933–34.

Two years had passed when, in February 1935, as the NSW players entered the dressing-room at the Brisbane Cricket Ground before their match with Queensland, they found a photograph of Archie on the dining table together with a bowl of fragrant roses – placed there by Phyllis Thomas to commemorate the second anniversary of their engagement. There was a momentary hush as the players dumped their cricket bags; unexpectedly it was a time for memories.

There were all sorts of reasons for remembering him. A boy from North Sydney remembered the trouble taken by Archie Jackson in 1930 after he had sent him an autograph book with the request that both Australian and West Indian teams should sign it. The book was lost, so the boy wrote again. Jackson bought a fresh book, had it signed, and kept up a cordial correspondence for the remaining months of his life.

The second coming of Trumper had been short-lived, but the course of cricket history was changed by a few degrees. When Jackson's summers were gone for ever, men, women and children grieved. A torrent of words came forth in the vain wish to do justice to the young man and his deeds. Then life went on again, almost as before, leaving only photographs, grey columns of prose, a few handwritten letters, and, over a plot of Australia's hard brown earth, a gravestone on which the inscription proclaims with beautiful simplicity: 'He played the game'.

BATTING STATISTICS

Balmain 1st XI	Ins.	N.O.	H.S.	Runs	Av.	100s
1924–25	12	4	41*	246	30.75	0
1925–26	18	1	129	670	39.41	1
1926–27	12	2	158	870	87.00	5
1927–28	6	2	110*	326	81.50	2
1928–29	4	0	79	177	44.25	0
1929–30	5	0	161	360	72.00	1
1930–31	2	0	106	115	57.50	1
1931–32	5	2	183	320	106.66	1
	64	11	183	3084	58.19	11

Northern Suburbs (Brisbane) 1st XI						
1932–33	7	4	124*	479	159.66	2

Sheffield Shield for New South Wales						
1926–27	11	3	104*	464	58.00	2
1927–28	9	0	131	360	40.00	2
1928–29	10	1	162	547	60.77	1
1929–30	5	0	82	193	38.60	0
1930–31	4	1	166	294	98.00	1
	39	5	166	1858	54.65	6

Test Matches						
1928–29 v England	4	0	164	276	69.00	1
1930 v England	2	0	73	74	37.00	0
1930–31 v West Indies	5	1	70*	124	31.00	0
	11	1	164	474	47.40	1

England Tour 1930 – All first-class matches other than Tests						
	33	3	118	1023	34.10	1

Other first-class matches in Australia						
1926–27	2	0	32	36	18.00	0
1927–28	1	0	104	104	104.00	1
1928–29	7	0	61	169	24.14	0
1929–30	5	1	182	437	109.25	2
1930–31	4	0	62	84	21.00	0
	19	1	182	830	46.11	3

New Zealand Tour 1927–28						
First-class matches	5	1	63	198	49.50	0
Other matches	6	0	110	276	46.00	1

INDEX

INDEX

INDEX